Tell me one thing
A Story of Two Mothers

CHARLOTTE M. SMITH

Book design by Mark F. Heiman

All of the events in this book are true, but the names of many individuals and places have been changed.

On the night Mark was to arrive I sat alone in our backyard and thought about the woman who had given birth to the little boy who was about to become our son. There was no way I could imagine giving up a child as she had done. I felt a deep connection to her, but I never expected to meet her.

머리말 *Foreword*

Imagine a young Korean woman in 1964 who has given birth in South Korea to a boy fathered by an American serviceman. The whereabouts of this father are unknown. Because this boy is a racially mixed child, his mother was disowned by her parental family. She is ordered to remove her name from the family register. Her son is labeled a *honhyul*, a non-person. As such, he is subject to discrimination, as is his mother, yet he is loved and cared for by this mother and grandmother, as best they could in such circumstances. By the time he was almost six and nearing school age and because the mother knew her son could never go to school, never even become a citizen, she agonized over the prospect of her son's future if he were to remain in this society. South Korea in 1970 was still struggling from years of warfare and civil strife, piled on top of colonial status (1910–45) under the Japanese and was then seeking a newly emerging identity, trying to honor its own traditions within a modern world. At such a time there are bound to be casualties, particularly among those who do not fit in.

Halfway across the world in mid-America a family of six is hoping to adopt a boy somewhat close in age to their youngest child. Having worked through an adoption agency, they are anticipating this Korean child's arrival with excitement. His soon-to-be adoptive mother, however, tried to imagine how this child's birth mother would survive the loss of her only child. As the adoptive mother sat alone under the stars the night he was to arrive on Northwest Airlines, she suddenly felt unexpectedly close to this unknown woman, trying to imagine, trying to understand this person's feelings, and what must be some of her questions: "Will I ever see him again? Will he miss me? Can I really let him go?" While these thoughts surfaced for the first time that evening, they continued to unfold over the years as she wondered how this Korean woman was doing, how she was coping with her loss. While never really knowing at this point of time, she kept this woman in her mind and heart. She never expected to meet this woman.

In May of 1970 a frightened, exhausted boy of nearly six arrives to become a member of a brand new family. This new experience was far from easy. Within the first year, he felt the sting of being called a "chink." The sense of being different in this society reminded him of similar treatment in Korea. In time he revealed an extraordinary resilience, and as he grew in self-confidence his peers learned to see his strength of character and generosity of spirit. He became the kind of young boy, for instance, who reached out to others who were bullied. His adaptation in this new and different culture amazed everyone. As he matured he sometimes spoke of suppressed memories about those first six years and later, when asked if he would ever like to visit Korea and even try to locate his "first" mother, he eventually said, "Yes." Instead of this step being a threat to his adoptive parents, they hoped that it would help him to knit together two segments—of his early years and his approaching manhood. It was a door they hoped he would want to open.

The writing of this story arose, to a large degree, from an attempt to assess the impact upon the birth mother of losing her only child. The experience of social ostracism, panic and finally loss of her son to an unknowable future was devastating. The feelings of the adoptive family were also about the child and what he went through in Korea and in his early years in Minnesota. There are few if any books that deal with the adoption of a six year-old Korean child. Most Korean adoptees are infants. Because of his age at adoption, the family actively sought to find his birth mother, though they did not commence this process until he was old enough to be part of the decision (shortly before college).

Their primary reason for trying to open this door was sensitivity to what this woman must have experienced, remaining in the dark for years about the existence of her child. From the beginning, they tried to imagine the extent of her loss, as well as how this new son was navigating his existence without fully understanding why he had been sent away. Rationally, he "knew," but emotionally, it remained an unanswerable question—until he finally met his birth mother again. The family's feelings were a leap of imagination: they sought to understand how the submerged demons of both mother and child have figured in their lives. To imagine how this birth mother and her child faced such loss was the impetus for this book.

Samuel Ingram,
A family friend

하나 *Chapter 1*

The grating, grinding sound of the cable, spewing out of the ship's hull jarred me out of a restless sleep. Even before I opened my eyes, my heart started pounding, and I felt as though I were plunging downward with the ship's anchor, through the darkness of the sea. Then I heard the thump of the heavy anchor settling onto the earth of the ocean's floor in the outer harbor of Pusan, South Korea.

I looked up at the bottom of the narrow bunk above my own. Our nineteen year old son, Mark, lay there, snoring gently, one of his hands visible, hanging over the edge of the mattress. Raising myself carefully on one elbow so as not to wake him, I peered into the semi-darkness of early dawn and glanced about the tiny stateroom.

On a nearby bed I could see my husband Cameron's form and hear his slow, deep breathing. Mark was Cameron's son, too, and with that loving realization, I began to waken fully and remembered why the three of us had boarded the ferry boat at Shimonoseki, a port city on the southwestern side of Japan, and headed for the destination we had just now reached. It was July, 1983, and we were bringing our son back to his native land, where we had found him thirteen years before.

Awakening slowly in these unfamiliar surroundings thousands of miles from home, I slowly became aware of why we had come this far. Mark had been ambivalent about the trip, wondering why his parents thought it was important for him to touch base with the first six years of his life, but eventually his curiosity triumphed over his doubts, anxiety and fears. As I lay still, cradled by the gentle motion of the moored ship,

I watched the early morning light dance about the room. Deciding to come on this trip had not been easy, but eventually we had decided it was worth the effort, time, and cost. Now, I could not help but wonder what lay ahead for us, especially for our son, in the next two weeks.

Easily lulled by this floating world, I dreamed my way back to the beginning days, thirteen years before, of our long and remarkable journey with Mark.

In a blustery mid-January morning in 1970, I was in our kitchen in Newberry, Minnesota, cleaning up after breakfast. The phone rang: Barbara Adams, our social worker from the adoption agency, was on the line.

"Good morning, Martha. I hope it's not too early to call, but I wanted to reach you as soon as possible. I have good news! Mr. Chung, the director of the Seoul agency, was in Minneapolis late yesterday. He brought folders on several Korean children. There are some that I think will interest you and Cameron. When do you think you could come to look at them?" With my heart pounding, I managed to respond, "I'll call Cameron and let you know." The rest of the day I floated!

The next morning we were silent on the hour's drive north from our town. Just before 10 a.m. we walked into the familiar low brick building on the outskirts of downtown Minneapolis. We had been there to attend pre-adoption seminars. A receptionist ushered us into a small room with one large window. Barbara Adams, a warm and sprightly woman, came in with about twenty folders and placed them in two piles on the table. Her wisdom had guided us through the adoption process over the past several months. "I'm so glad you could come this morning. Please take your time. I'll be in my office down the hall if you need me." She closed the door and left us alone.

Cameron pulled his chair forward, bent over the table and spread the contents of the top folder in front of him. I put on my reading glasses, slipped off my shoes and curled up in the high-back upholstered chair next to him. I reached for the folder on top of the second pile. In that peaceful place, we began the search for our fifth child.

Our oldest, Tim, had been drafted and was now stationed in New Mexico. Emily, our older daughter, worked in a restaurant in Florida, and Sarah, a senior in high school, was looking at colleges for the next year. Our seven-year-old son, Alex, had often wished out loud that he had a brother to play with. Instead of just smiling when Alex brought it up, Cameron and I began to be enthusiastic about the idea. Neither of us wanted Alex to grow up feeling like an only child. Because of our ages, the possibility of adoption loomed large.

Adoption had already played a major role in the creation of our family. When Cameron and I married, he had adopted my three children, aged eight, eleven and thirteen. In 1970, both of us were approaching our mid-forties. We knew that within the United States adoption was a difficult, long, and often frustrating, procedure—nearly impossible for people our age. From the beginning we cast our eyes across the Pacific. It was a natural affinity. For a decade Cameron had been teaching in the field of Asian religions at Calhoun College in Newberry. We had lived in Japan at various periods during those years, while Cameron taught or pursued research interests. In the fall of 1969, upon returning from the summer in Japan, we approached one of the large adoption agencies in Minneapolis, knowing that it had recently begun to accelerate overseas adoptions, especially from Korea.

We were soon filling out forms and more forms. We gathered references from friends, bankers, our lawyer, and our minister. Medical records were sent off. Fingerprints were taken at our local police station. After several months, the adoption agency announced that our documents were in order.

Cameron and I attended pre-adoption meetings with other parents interested in adopting international and/or interracial children. Together we discussed the meaning of parenthood, attitudes about nationality and race, and our expectations. The group considered problems these children might face—within the family, the school, and the community, both immediately, and in the future.

We met separately with Barbara Adams, whose voice and manner put us at ease. As we sat across the table from her at our first meeting, she encouraged us to share our hopes, and to be specific about what we were looking for and what we could provide.

"Think about your other children, your lifestyle. Take into account what you like to do and where you live. Don't be rigid—but do have priorities. You've probably thought about this already. I just want to emphasize how important your input is."

"Martha and I have thought and talked a great deal about this," Cameron said. "We know we would like, if possible, a Korean-American child, someone whose birth father was an American stationed in Korea. We have learned that a decent life for these children is next to impossible in Korea. And, we would *definitely* like a boy.

"Our two oldest are away from home, and our high-school senior will be off to college in the fall. But Alex, almost seven, is a first grader, and we'd like the two young boys to grow up together. We hope they will be close enough in age to do things with each other, and will have the possibility of a close relationship. So a boy somewhere between the ages of four and six would be ideal."

Barbara nodded. "Good, that helps a lot. What other things are important to you?"

My turn. "We think it's very important for a child to have a close, sustained relationship with at least one adult during the early, formative years. We hope our child will have experienced some sense of family life beyond what is possible in an institution."

Barbara nodded. "Yes, especially when a child is the age you are thinking about. These are valuable things to keep in mind."

She jotted a few notes, attaching them to the top of her clipboard. Then she looked up at us, smiling, "We'll let you know when the next batch of folders arrives from Korea. I hope it won't be too many weeks before you hear from us."

Now, a few weeks later, with the folders in front of us, Cameron and I each read silently, completely absorbed. Each of the folders contained information on boys aged three to six and a half years, the range we had favored on our application. Two of the children were full Koreans, but most were *honhyul*, children of mixed-racial background.

What happened to me that particular morning was profound. Though it had entered my thoughts fleetingly in the months past, suddenly, as I read the folders, this reality hit me hard. We were looking for a new son to be part of our family. But deep in my heart, I imagined a mother, somewhere in Korea, giving up a child, a child she had birthed and nurtured for years: now, because of conditions beyond her control, this mother has given up her child to new, unknown parents in some other part of the world. How...oh how, I wondered, how this could have happened?

Just then Cameron murmured something, and I looked up at him. "Ah, wait a minute!" I knew by the tone of his voice and the way his eyes engaged mine that something had clicked. He said in a quiet voice, "This may be our boy!" I put down the folder I was reading and reached for the one Cameron handed me.

The photograph at the top of the first page was of a child with large, dark brown, deep-set eyes. The slight tilt of his head, the suggestion of a smile, hinted of shyness. I held the picture up close. He was looking straight at me. I glanced quickly at Cameron who was watching me as I began to read the folder.

"Young Ho is a child of Korean-Caucasian parentage. He has fair complexion with dark-brown hair and Caucasian-shaped eyes. His relationship with his mother and grandmother seems to be confident and close, but he demonstrates maturity in his independence from them. He is now aware of the fact of being a child of mixed parentage and knows that his father is an American who has not been reached since his birth. His mother and grandmother realize that they will not be capable of providing the child with proper continued care and education. They know he will face many problems if he stays in Korea because he is different. They have come to plan on adoptive placement of the child for his better future."

I got up from my chair and stood by the window. It had started to snow, and as I watched the white crystals swirl about in the wind and settle on the ground. Inside me, whirling emotions were also coming to a resting place. Something had happened to me, as it had to Cameron, when I gazed at the picture of that small face. I turned back to the table and saw that Cameron was still, watching me, and waiting for my reaction: Our feelings were the same. Our closeness, in that moment, was transparent.

My eyes went back to the photograph. From some deep place within me, a distant memory stirred: it was strangely connected to the memory of my first gaze upon a newborn babe nestled in my arms.

Cameron and I tried to remain calm and open, but we were overwhelmed with excitement. To choose an infant would be difficult enough, and yet we were attempting to single out *one* child, out of many, to be our son. This was a boy who had already lived part of his life, a life very different from life as we knew it.

We studied the remaining folders carefully, trying to visualize each small person as part of our family. After rereading the material in the *maybe* pile, we talked seriously about two or three of the children, but I slowly added those folders to the pile of ones we had set aside. I felt sad as my hand came to rest on top of these folders. Each of these little children had entered our lives momentarily, and then we had let them go.

"Oh, Cameron! This is so *hard!*"

"I know. Each of those boys deserves the chance of a better life. It's not easy, not easy at all." We sat quietly for a few moments, as if marking our brief encounter with those young lives. Cameron said softly, "But, hopefully, we can give one boy a fresh start."

Our eyes fell on the single folder we had set aside from the rest. We read it once more, out loud. Carefully we examined every clue. His age was perfect—five and a half. But most engaging were the comments of those who had observed him when he was brought to the agency in Seoul for a ten-day period.

"He is a cheerful, active boy who warms up to people easily. From the first day of entry into the Home, he got along well with adults and children, as if he had been here before. This child prefers active outdoor play and likes group games. He likes to sing and particularly enjoys machinery toys."

The decision was crystal clear. We wanted Young Ho to be our son!

We gathered up the folders and went down the hall to Barbara Adams' office. Her door was open. We stood just outside as she finished talking on the phone. She glanced at our faces and responded with a knowing smile. She put the phone down and we announced with joy and in unison, "We've found him!"

Chapter 2

There was movement on the top bunk. I opened my eyes, and saw Cameron dressing. "Time to get up, you two. The ship is moving." Soon the three of us stood on deck at the starboard rail as our ferry glided toward its berth in the inner harbor. It had been Mark's idea to make the trip by ship. "When you fly into big cities," he said, "it always seems so abrupt, and all the airports look about the same."

The sun was sinking when we left Japan the evening before. As we moved slowly past tankers and cargo ships and glided through the miles of narrow harbor channels, we watched the rocky shorelines of innumerable small islands disappear in the dusk.

The uneventful passage across the Korean Strait was an important transition. For Mark, this was a valuable threshold, the space separating the known from the almost-forgotten. How much would he remember? Mark was about to enter the world of his earliest days, a world long-buried and nearly forgotten. He'd left his home in America, where he had found acceptance, love, and security. Ahead lay uncertain connections, possible entanglements, and, no doubt, painful memories.

The ship's journey linked the world I knew with a culture as yet unknown to me, but one I wanted to experience and understand. I wanted to feel and absorb the differences and the commonalities. I wanted to find the solid base, the anchor that was part of our son, for Mark's sake.

Now, as we stood at the ship's railing a heavy mist rose from the glassy green water blurring the shoreline. Its beauty was haunting. In earlier centuries the Korean people had called their land, *Chosun*, meaning "morning calm." Mark was right: we would have missed this moment had we flown into Seoul.

Yet still, as I looked out, I wondered if we had made the right decision in coming. I caught Cameron's eye…made myself smile and crossed my fingers as I nodded a small "yes!" or "let's hope so!"

The ferry's shrill whistle announced our arrival at the pier, black smoke belching from the stack. As the mist soon cleared, we saw that we were surrounded by ships from around the world, docked at the long quays that lined the narrow inlet in Pusan. The noise of cranes reaching into the bellies of the transports blended with the longshoremen's shouts. Large vehicles spewing noxious gases lined up to receive goods to take to distant places in South Korea. Everywhere, people scurried back and forth along the docks.

For nearly an hour we waited in line while a sleepy-eyed immigration officer processed the fifty or so passengers into Korea. After the first half hour of waiting, Mark turned to us and said, impatiently, "I don't know. This is a bummer." Frustration crept across his face, revealing, perhaps, some of the inner anxiety he must be feeling. He added, half under his breath, "Now that we're here, let's get going!"

"It won't be long now," Cameron said hopefully as I looked for some edibles in my purse and passed them to Mark.

After the drawn-out immigration ordeal, we began an all-day trip on a half-filled, no-frills bus that stopped frequently between Pusan and Seoul. The roads we traveled on were generally narrow, bumpy, and often curving.

Life bustled in the small cities and villages we wove through. Cars were scarce and many men rode bicycles, honking their rubber horns frequently to scatter children or others. No one seemed hurried.

We watched young mothers in long colorful skirts, their infants or toddlers strapped on their backs or fronts, shopping in small stalls along the main street. Each village had an open food market filled with colorful fruits and vegetables, dried mushrooms, and large jars of *kim-chi*, a garlic-laced cabbage.

At one stop, five or six women were talking in small groups while their rosy-cheeked children played together at their feet. The children's faces, which were beautiful, with their dark eyes, black hair, and warm, glowing complexions intrigued me.

I saw one young mother, crouched at the edge of the group, her arms around her young child huddled in front of her. They were watching the children at play. From the bus seat ahead of ours Mark was watching them, too. As the bus pulled forward, Mark turned in his seat to watch them a bit longer. I wondered, was he remembering when he, Young Ho, watched with his mother while other children played, when they did not want him or his mother to join them?

On the bus we observed our fellow passengers and listened to their incomprehensible chatter. "Does any of it sound familiar, Mark?" Cameron asked. Mark's head signaled a *no*.

As we moved along the road, I remembered what Sheila, an American friend, had told us when she visited us in Japan during the summer of 1969. Sheila, a social worker concerned with international adoptions, had just returned from touring several social service agencies on the Korean peninsula.

"The plight of Korean children fathered by American servicemen would tear at your heart," she told us. "These men had fought there during the war or are now part of the United Nations peacekeeping force. The racially mixed children are called *honhyul*, meaning 'non-person'. Because they're easily identifiable as not being 'pure' Koreans, they're badly discriminated against. Adults and children taunt them and call them names. Usually their mothers are ostracized as well. In Korea the father must register a child for school so no education is available to these children. No decent jobs are open to them. They can't even become citizens in the country of their birth. If they survive, these children become vulnerable to the most unsavory elements of society."

As Cameron and I had listened, the sadness on his face mirrored my own. "Korea is one of the most insular countries in the world," Cameron said, "among the most insular. Koreans are tenacious in preserving, holding onto, what they claim as their own. They cherish what is pure and untainted by outside influences."

Sheila nodded. "Those attitudes come from experiences of oppressive colonial rule, outside political dominance, and deprivation of an ancient and vibrant culture. The Japanese colonial regime even attempted to strip the Korean language from them. In recent decades, all these things have made Koreans overly protective."

I understood, but my insides ached. "Did you see large numbers of mixed-racial children when you were there?" I had asked.

"Yes," Sheila told us, "mostly infants, but some young children too. Outside of the extended family, adoption is not part of the Korean way. However, there have been an increasing number of overseas adoptions by Americans and Europeans. In fact, my trip's goal was to try and find ways to facilitate overseas adoption of some of these children.

"The children are brought to one of the social service homes, often soon after birth, by mothers who are desperate. They have no other place to turn. If a child is not born into an established family—or if the child is somehow different—it is banished, excluded. Its mother, also."

Questions we asked ourselves twenty some years before, when we first thought about adopting an overseas child, now surfaced again as we continued our long bus ride:

"Is it right to remove a child from familiar surroundings and his own racial background and bring him to a very different culture, and to separate a child from his mother or other family members?

"Does the fact that America would offer the child rights and opportunities not possible in Korea, make it okay?

"What will life be like for this child in a brand new world?

"Will it be especially difficult for an *older* child to make the adjustment? In later years will the child have trouble answering the question, 'Who am I?'

"Are we taking into account all the changes that will happen throughout our family?" we mused. We answered *yes* and *no*, and often *sometimes* and *maybe*.

Our heads acknowledged the risks; our hearts compelled us to move forward.

Our Pusan-to-Seoul bus pulled into a restaurant at the side of the road, and along with the twenty or so other passengers we went inside the small building to have lunch. Tables covered with bright yellow plastic cloths were crowded into a minimal space. A few older men were sitting at a round table in an alcove sipping tea when we entered. They looked at us—especially at Mark—with curiosity and watched us as we sat down at one of the small tables. The menu, written in Korean, was of no use to us. When the waiter came to our table, Cameron pointed to a steaming bowl being brought to a nearby table and held up three fingers. In a few minutes three bowls were set before us. It was a hot, spicy concoction of *kimchi*, chili, and grilled fish served over rice. We detected curious stares in our direction from others in the restaurant. Cameron said in a low voice, "I'm sure not many foreigners travel on this bus route."

"And they're trying to figure me out, I'll bet," Mark said into his dish.

I tried not to pay attention to their attentiveness, and instead chattered about our first hours in Korea. Halfway through our simple meal, Mark lifted his head and glanced about. I was aware that a dozen or so of the customers continued staring at us, mostly at Mark. Whatever Mark might have been feeling, I need not have worried. Our son, savoring the last of his meal, raised his head, looked around and then fixed on an elderly man at a nearby table, looking directly into his eyes. And then, much to our surprise, a warm smile broke across Mark's face. The man smiled back and the two women at his table joined in with murmurs of approval. Mark had taken his first step across the bridge leading him back to his long-forgotten home.

During the remaining four hours on the bus, as we continued in a northwesterly direction across the Korean peninsula toward Seoul, our relationship with the other passengers became less strained. When we passed a beautiful mountain or an ancient temple, someone on the bus would point to us and then to the side of the bus where we should look. Once we passed a farmer pushing an enormous load of vegetables on a two-wheeled wagon, and our fellow riders turned to us, speaking excitedly.

In Seoul, at the end of our long bus trip our fellow passengers waved goodbye and showed surprise when, by previous arrangement, we were met and warmly welcomed by Professor Kim, a Korean whom we had known quite well in America. For a few years he and his family were part of our college community, and we were delighted to see him again. That first night he took us to a *yogwan*, a typical Korean inn. We had a warm visit with our friend as we ate the evening meal served on small tables in our room. Afterward, the three of us walked Professor Kim to a main thoroughfare where he could get a cab.

On the way back to our inn, we passed through a working-class neighborhood where gaudy, neon signs in Korean script competed for shoppers' attention. Food stands were overflowing with aromatic melons, peaches, and tomatoes. Five or six children tossed a ball in the narrow, stone-paved street. Every other doorway led to a place to eat—tiny tables or floor mats catering to hungry passersby. At one, a grandmother tossed heavy cardboard discs of different colors to children outside. At another, a woman squatted next to huge woven baskets of flour and grains. A baby clad only in a nightshirt straddled its mother's back. Under a street lamp, an old man and a young boy sat backwards on small chairs, their fingers moving smooth, black and white stones back and forth on the *Go* game board set on a small table between them.

As we passed through this scene, it was obvious that eyes were upon us... two Caucasian adults with a young man easily identified as a *hon-hyul*. Two young children ran to their mothers and turning toward us, nodded in Mark's direction. Another woman nearby, exchanging words with her neighbors, watched us closely as we passed by. A quick glance at Mark revealed his discomfort... his memories of being an outsider must have flooded in upon him. As we approached the end of the street, Mark stopped and turned around to view the scene in its entirety. Without turning back to us, he said, "We lived in a hut and there was no paved road... and I didn't even have... one friend to play with."

The three of us walked back to our inn, silently. Sleep did not come easily.

For the next few days, Professor Kim guided us through Seoul. We viewed the Great South Gate, built in 1396, and walked along wide boulevards bordering the Han River. We roamed the museums and palaces, viewing the exquisite, luminous celadon vases and ceremonial ware, as well as the intricate craftsmanship of metalwork and jewelry. We lingered in front of the centuries-old ink landscape drawings with their delicate shading and subdued color, imbued with the beauty of the natural world and man's oneness with it.

Mark was not to be hurried as we marveled at such treasures. He didn't want to miss a thing. After two and a half hours of examining the many displays, Professor Kim suggested we have tea, but Mark declined. He went back to the exhibit of ancient bronze bells.

As we walked the streets, present-day Seoul was inescapably upon us. We watched and listened to the noisy construction of the subway system and high-rise buildings late into the evening hours. The sprawling, exploding city was preparing for the Asian games in 1986, three years hence, a prelude to the hosting of the Olympics in 1988. The ugliness and energy of a burgeoning metropolis were everywhere. Mark might claim all this as part of his heritage—the past and the present of the Korean people—and I wondered if he did.

One evening, we invited Professor Kim, his wife, and their two young daughters to join us for a buffet at our hotel. Delectable Korean dishes were spread out on a large table, tempting us. Besides *kimchi* and various pickled delicacies, we ate grilled fish on a stick, oxtail soup, bean sprout salad, mushrooms and rice seasoned with sesame, ginger, chili, and liberal portions of garlic. More than once Mark returned to the serving table, filling his plate each time. He asked Professor Kim the Korean name of the different foods he was eating.

Mark seemed as comfortable in this setting as if he were back home in Minnesota sitting at our table, eating spaghetti or hamburger in a bun. Did the taste and the aroma of those ethnic dishes awaken memories of other meals many years ago, which he had shared with his mother? As I watched him, I imagined it might be so.

Cameron and I, accustomed to the four-sided wooden chopsticks of Japan, struggled with the round, embossed silver ones common in Korea. We were trying to cope with the unfamiliar, while Mark, who used these tools as deftly as our Korean friends, once again seemed to have become Young Ho. Perfectly at ease, he engaged the young girls in a bit of conversation and then he asked Professor Kim about his research.

샛 *Chapter 3*

Years before, at an early meeting with Barbara Adams at the Minneapolis Adoption Agency, she suggested that we give our new son an American name. "It will help the child feel more a part of his new family." Before he came to us we decided to call our son "Mark" after Cameron's grandfather who had come as an immigrant from Scotland a century ago.

After our adoption papers were in order we had expected to wait nine months to a year for Mark to arrive. To our astonishment, on April 14, 1970—three months after our trip to the adoption agency in Minneapolis—we received this communiqué, special delivery:

"All papers have been processed for the release of your adoptive son. You may expect him to arrive on May 3rd. Your Minneapolis agency will be in touch."

I called Minneapolis immediately. "Barbara, how could this be? We're flabbergasted. He'll be here in less than three weeks!"

She laughed. "We've just received word ourselves. We think the clearance came through quickly because of his age. We're happy for you and for him. When we receive details of his arrival, I'll call. Good luck! You'll have a busy couple of weeks."

She was right.

Cameron and I painted the bedroom that Alex and Mark would share. Sarah and Alex helped us assemble new bunk beds. We purchased clothes. Alex wanted to get him a stuffed animal. He decided on a large, soft brown, malleable monkey that could hang from his tail or his limbs. Alex also picked out a new toothbrush—a purple one—and put it between Sarah's and his own in the bathroom. Packages arrived from family members in New England: a hand-knit sweater, Richard Scarry's *Picture Dictionary*, a game of parcheesi.

Friends got together and bought Mark a bright red tricycle with a large, squeezable horn.

The waiting was almost over. Mark's plane was due in Minneapolis very early the next morning… at 1:50 a.m.!

In the late afternoon, Alex practiced catching tennis balls in our driveway while waiting for his dad to come home from work. Ivan (our large black poodle) sat on his haunches close by, ready to retrieve misses. When Alex saw his father pedaling around the corner on his faded black Raleigh, he ran to meet him.

"Dad, can we still practice before supper?"

"Sure," said Cameron, "I'll get my glove."

"Yippee! I thought we wouldn't have time tonight."

"Be out in a minute," Cameron yelled over his shoulder. He came through the screen door to the kitchen where I was preparing supper. We stood silently, looking at one another across the kitchen. My teeth pressed down on my lower lip, my instinctive response when words elude me. As I turned again to the sink, Cameron moved to me and put his arm around my shoulder.

"Sorry I didn't make it home for lunch. How's the day been for you?" he asked.

I practically whispered my reply. "I've tried to keep busy. Lots of people have called to say they're thinking of us. I keep thinking of things he might need. I've been to the store twice. Actually, it's been kind of crazy—unreal."

"I've had trouble concentrating myself," Cameron admitted. "Finally I told my students what was going on in our lives today. You should have heard the clapping! Everybody was shouting out congratulations!"

Then he hugged me quickly. "I'm going out with Alex for a bit."

Before long, Sarah arrived home from her flute lesson and joined me in the kitchen. She filled Ivan's dog dish and put it down on his mat. She poured milk for Alex and iced tea for the rest of us. Flopping down into a chair at the breakfast table, Sarah smiled out the window and said, "I just don't ever remember being this excited except when Alex was born—but this is different, isn't it, Mom?" I nodded and for the first time it really hit me: I would not be his first mother!

Soon Cameron and Alex came in for supper. We ate on the back porch, a place we have cherished for meals, reading and talking together. In our busy lives, it was a haven that helped us keep in touch with ourselves and each other. From the porch we had the best view of the Japanese garden at the rear of our property—a place of peace and serenity. This garden had been designed by a close friend, following his years of apprenticeship in Japan. Low green plants bordered ancient rocks along with a central Scotch pine, and a wide, pebbled stream bed. "I hope Mark will like it, too," I found myself thinking.

Sarah ate and left the table to study. Alex pushed back his chair and announced that he was going to the park.

"When do I gotta be home?" he asked, bouncing the back of his chair.

"Seven-thirty," I said. "Remember, you'll be going to bed early to get some sleep before we go to the airport."

"Yeah, Mom," he answered automatically.

Cameron reached over, affectionately caught hold of Alex, spun him around, and perched him on a knee. His arms slid around Alex's waist, holding him quietly for a moment. His cheek touched the softness of his son's.

"You know," he said, "seven and a half years ago, there was this same kind of excitement around here. *You* were about to arrive on that bitter cold January night. Tim, Emily and Sarah whooped around here like crazy when I called them from the hospital."

Alex's back relaxed against his father's chest. It curved in to accept the full warmth of his dad's embrace.

"I wish Mark were here already. Where is he now?"

"Somewhere over the Pacific Ocean, headed for Seattle, we hope," I answered.

"I wonder if he's scared." Alex looked at me, then turned around and glanced up at his dad.

"What do *you* think?" Cameron asked.

"Yeah, I think Mark's scared. I am, too… a little." Alex sat quietly for a moment. Then sitting up straight in his Dad's lap, he shifted gears. "Say, Mom, can I *really* stay home from school tomorrow?"

I smiled at him. "It's all set. We'll both be home. In fact, I won't be teaching for a couple of weeks."

"I just wish I didn't have to go to bed so early tonight!" Alex exclaimed.

"Maybe you'd rather meet your brother in the morning," Cameron teased.

Wiggling off his dad's lap, Alex made a silly grimace. "No way," he shouted as he slammed the screen door, hopped on his bicycle, and headed for the park.

"Our seven-year-old has been dancing his way through the last several days," said Cameron. "It's gonna be a trick getting him calmed down!"

"His dad has a way," I thought as we cleared the table. "I think I'll leave it to you." Cameron headed upstairs to his office. I called after him. "I'm going to take a walk while you get Alex to bed. And I'll call Northwest at nine-thirty to check on the flight."

My adrenaline level surged, and my rapid heartbeat began to energize my every move. The supper dishes flew in and out of the dishwater. I scrubbed the Formica counters, nearly wiping out the design. Though I felt myself moving at a quickened pace, the clock seemed to turn backward. It struck me suddenly that I'd been here before. As the delivery of each of my other children became imminent, the hours had seemed to crawl.

I knew I needed time by myself. I draped my navy cardigan over my shoulders and put Ivan on his leash. We walked down the familiar paved road leading to the two connecting lakes on campus.

That evening Ivan was my perfect companion, a friend who would comfort me without asking too many questions; I was asking myself all the questions I could handle. Could I be an adequate mother to a six-year-old boy I had never laid eyes on? A boy who had lived those crucial, early years calling someone else 'Mother'? A boy who grew up in a far distant, far different place? A boy who spoke only Korean?

Then I remembered the photograph.

Ivan and I crossed the small wooden bridge between the lakes and headed onto the narrow, wooded path that winds along the water's edge. Here and there hepaticas, with their lobed leaves and delicate pink flowers, peeked above the protective ground cover. The tree frogs sang in concert, their high-pitched drone in dubious harmony with the deep, sonorous "jug-o-rums" of the bullfrogs. One of them hit the water with a plop when Ivan sniffed too close to its perch. We watched a beaver trailing undulating lines of luminous water as it headed for the opposite shore. My breathing became slower, deeper. I imagined the next time I stood at the edge of the lake that Alex and Mark would be there, too.

I continued along the brook, grateful that Cameron was getting Alex bedded down. The western sky glowed with dimming shafts of light. The beauty and the soft evening air calmed me as I walked slowly along the path. I had temporarily brought my emotions under control. Temporarily, I needed to remain calm, but at moments I was nearly overwhelmed by the feelings rising within me. I tingled with happiness. I felt light-headed, giddy. I wanted to dance. I wanted to cry. What if something went wrong? What if he didn't like us or our house or our town?

From Seoul, Korea, a teeming metropolis of nearly four million, he was coming to a small Minnesota community barely over ten thousand! Across time zones and seemingly infinite space, this small child would soon arrive in an alien land.

I tried to envision this town as he would see it for the first time. I walked the streets in my mind, pausing here and there. In my imagination I became a six-year-old for whom everything would be not only new but very strange. No face was familiar; I couldn't speak the language; even my name had changed and the only mother I ever knew was nowhere in sight.

I struggled to shift gears. I wanted and hoped Mark would learn to love this place as our other children did. It was an easy place to live in and to love. Early citizens had had vision enough to build wide streets and plant hundreds of stately elms alongside them. In their maturity, those trees now formed graceful arches above the pavement.

Kids pedaled their bikes from one end of town to the other—to the neighborhood schools, playing fields, swimming pool, parks. Stopping at Bridgeman's for ice cream or the bakery for a cinnamon roll, a child might hear a friendly adult call his name and ask how school was going.

The main street ran parallel to a lovely little river with three modest bridges. Children loved the park across from the flourmill where they watched the rush of water over the dam, especially in spring. An overworked Carnegie library, in the center of town, drew children in large numbers to discover books and innovative programs.

Tomorrow, I mused, this would become Mark's hometown, too.

Ivan and I walked back to our house... I felt calmness deep inside and mused softly to myself—"I think I'm ready."

I stood in our kitchen, the phone cradled at my ear. It was 9:35 and the Northwest operator had just put me on hold. The kitchen radio was tuned to the evening symphony concert. I leaned against the cabinet, and took some long, deep breaths.

I looked around the room, at the memorabilia of our everyday lives: family snapshots and photos of friends, favorite quotes, notices of up-coming events on the bulletin board, Alex's drawing of a baseball game on the refrigerator door. On the wall across from where I stood was a favorite picture, the "Meeting of St. Anthony and St. Paul" by the 15th-century Italian artist Sassetta. Painted in subtle earth tones and framed in a soft burnished gold, it showed two monks on a wooded path greet-ing one another in a welcoming embrace.

Minutes later, the operator came back on the line. The plane carry-ing our son had landed in Seattle twenty minutes earlier, she informed me. It would arrive on time in Minneapolis. Then she asked, "Are you meeting a child from Korea?"

"Yes," I told her.

In a warm voice she added, "These flights are the most special ones we have. Best wishes and good luck!"

Surprised, I uttered, "Thanks, thanks very much." I went two steps at a time upstairs to my husband's office. He looked up from his desk. "It's on time! The plane's on time, Cameron." He stood and we held each other.

I peeked in Tim's old bedroom. Alex was asleep in his big brother's bed, his small body turned toward the wall. On my way downstairs, I paused in front of the bedroom with the bunk beds that Alex and Mark would share. Laid out on the floor was a large foam-rubber pad with two sleeping bags and pillows on top. Alex and I had brought them up from a closet in the basement when he came home from school. Barbara Adams had suggested that the first night I stay beside Mark on the floor where he was used to sleeping. Blue and red plaid pajamas, size eight, lay folded on top of one of the pillows. Next to them Alex had carefully placed the large stuffed monkey.

Sarah appeared beside me, a plate of cold leftovers in her hand. Looking down at the sleeping bags, she said in a hushed voice, "I'll bet nobody around here gets much sleep tonight!"

Three hours to go. I went downstairs, turned up the radio in the kitchen, and moved out of the porch door to the stone steps at the edge of the terrace. The stars were bright. In the darkness, strains of music from the kitchen radio blended with the fragrant spring air. I looked up from the steps where I sat and watched a small plane humming its way across the sky, a red beacon pulsating through the night. Mark was up there, too, somewhere in the vastness, on the final stage of his first-ever flight. I wondered what he was thinking and feeling.

Yesterday he was there; very soon he will be here. Yesterday he was Young Ho Chae. Before the sun comes up he will be Mark Cameron McKay!

Suddenly, I found myself thinking not about the little boy who was within hours of joining our family, not about our other children, not about myself, but about the woman who had, only yesterday, said a final farewell to her almost-six-year-old son. How had she found the courage to let him go? How had this day dawned for her? Had she given birth to him to have him taken away? What would she do when the sun came up tomorrow? And, for all the tomorrows the rest of her life?

I thought of this woman releasing her child to the unknown. As I waited to embrace him into our lives, I glowed from an experience akin to birth. For her, the last day of their life together had to have been like a death—a shattering and final separation. And then came a vision unexpectedly of a shadowy image looking out into the darkness.

My joy still existed, yet I felt so deeply for this woman, my son's first mother. Her sorrow added a new dimension to my anticipation. That night, looking up at the bright stars of our universe, I became inextricably linked to a woman whom I would not meet for fourteen years.

넛 *Chapter 4*

It was 12:15 a.m. Time to go. I woke Alex and helped him into his clothes. Cameron got him settled on pillows in the back of the station wagon. Sarah sprawled across the back seat. I sat beside Cameron up front. We were quiet with anticipation.

Our headlights pierced the blackness as we drove north on Highway 3, through the unseen rolling farmland, into Farley, on to Rosewood. We could see only as far ahead as that beam of light on the road, nothing more. The foot soldiers of ancient Greece with lamps on their shoes had only enough light to illuminate their next step. For us, too, it was—and would be—one step at a time.

A half hour later we crossed the Minnesota River and wound around to the airport road. My stomach was whirling. Except for a few cars and the bright terminal lights ahead, the airport seemed deserted.

I turned toward the back seat. "Are you awake, Sarah? Alex, we're almost there."

We found a parking space close to the terminal. I passed around peanut butter crackers and milk. Alex came to. Sarah woke, but remained quiet. Cameron was alert. I was floating. Over and over, my heart whispered, "I can't believe this is happening. A new son, a brother, and a grandchild. A little boy is joining our family! Please, God, please help him to like us."

Once inside the terminal, we headed for the blue concourse. The clock read 1:30 a.m. The plane, due in twenty minutes, was on time. At Gate 15 about forty persons, including a few children, stood in small groups. A woman went to the microphone and spoke in a warm, friend-ly voice.

"Dear friends, we have eight boys and five girls arriving on this flight. All but four are infants. When the other passengers have left the plane, we invite you parents to come onto the plane to meet your daughters and sons. The children have been cared for by members of the armed forces and other volunteers on the twenty-two-hour trip from Seoul. Remember, your children will be very tired. Good luck to each and every one of you!"

She passed among us, handing out documents, offering words of encouragement. I turned to a couple standing close by. "Excuse me, but how will we know which child is ours?" I asked. The man looked me straight in the eyes, put a hand on my shoulder, and said "Don't worry! You will know!"

Then came a whir of sound and movement. Alex rushed to the window facing the tarmac. Everyone else moved in the same direction. The low, steady roar of engines filled the space. The lights of the approaching plane, coming nearer, penetrated the darkness. The ground crew beck-oned the nose of the monstrous 747 toward its docking area. Flashlights arced into the night, held by iridescent-garbed men luring the eerie gi-ant forward. Suddenly the great engines stopped. In the brief hush that followed, the tense muscles in my neck shoulders miraculously melted away. I was calmed by the wonder of what was about to take place.

We waited as regular passengers exited the plane. A few lingered in the waiting area to watch the impending drama.

"What if he's not on the plane?" Alex suddenly asked, looking up at us.

"He is, don't worry," Cameron assured him.

We heard our names called. "We'll be back in a few minutes," Cameron said to Sarah and Alex, who, like the other children, had to wait in the lobby to meet their new brother or sister. I walked as if in a trance toward the ramp.

As we approached the plane, we heard some crying as parents met their brand-new children. The stewardess asked our names, checked her documents, and said, "Your son is waiting for you. He's with an American soldier back at the exit area." She pointed down the aisle.

We walked a few steps. Next to the uniformed soldier in front of us were two boys standing side-by-side, hands locked together. Large postcard-sized tags with their American family's names were pinned to each shirt. Both boys were wide-eyed, and unsmiling. They looked terribly frightened.

The tall Black-Asian child had a round face and tight curly hair. The smaller boy was not much taller than a yardstick. He stared at us. He was our son.

He wore a royal blue turtleneck, short black pants, white stockings, and very small moccasins. Thick brown bangs highlighted eyes as dark as his hair. His small angular face was the color of an overripe peach, with the chin held high, the thin lips tightly shut, no hint of a smile. His chin quivered.

I wanted to gather this beautiful, exhausted child into my arms, but something told me not to.

"Hello," I said summoning my kindest voice. "Welcome," echoed Cameron softly. "We're so happy you're here, Mark." No response.

The new parents of the tall boy appeared, and the soldier led him to them. Cameron reached for our son's hand, but he kept it stiffly by his side. In his other hand he carried a red toy car. That and the small cloth satchel over his shoulder were all he had with him. The soldier said goodbye to him in Korean and told him to go along with us.

He was between Cameron and me as we walked back to Gate 15 where Sarah and Alex waited, holding hands. "Hi, Mark," said Alex. Sarah smiled. "We're glad to see you." Each sounded shy and awkward. Both of them had brought Mark a small gift. Alex presented a Matchbox truck; Sarah offered him a book. Mark took them and put them in his satchel.

No need to pick up baggage—there wasn't any. So we headed toward the parking lot. Mark moved steadily, stiffly, soberly, alongside his new family. On the path to our car, a low rope cordoned off broken pavement. Without warning, Mark changed his pace and jumped over it quickly, giving no heed to the cars heading for the exit gate. Cameron reached him and firmly took his hand.

In the car Mark sat on the edge of the back seat. As I perched next to him I watched his hands grip the back of the front seat. He stared ahead, his back straight and stiff. Cameron found music on the radio and lowered the volume.

"Is Mark okay?" Sarah, seated on my other side, whispered.

"He's exhausted, he's feeling jet lag, and everything is absolutely new to him, but he'll be okay," I said to reassure her—and myself.

Halfway home, Mark's head dropped forward, jerked back, dropped again. I gently put my arms around his shoulders, hoping to ease his head onto my lap. He didn't give an inch. Two miles from home he finally fell over in a heap, his head collapsed on my legs.

When, moments later, the car door opened in our driveway, Mark bolted to an upright position. I felt his shoulders move up and down, trembling. His breathing was labored and spasmodic. No longer could he hold back. He began to cry, then sob. Every time he tried to catch his breath, the sounds heaved forward from deep inside him. Cameron carried Mark upstairs to the room with the sleeping bags. The new pajamas were set aside.

He cried continuously for four and a half hours.

I lay beside him on the floor, gently rubbing his back. Sometimes he cried out for his mother, "O-mo-ni," or his grandmother, "Hal mo-ni." Each mournful sob pierced my heart. I ached inside for him and for myself. I prayed that comforting sleep would overtake this helpless little child.

It finally did. At 8 a.m., as the May sun brightened the room where he lay, Mark's heaving breaths shifted to the deep rhythmic melody of profound sleep. At that moment for me, it was the most beautiful sound in the universe.

Shortly after 4 p.m., I heard a noise upstairs. Walking into the hall, I looked up the staircase to see Mark in his now-crumpled clothes with his chin resting on the banister. He was swinging one foot back and forth. I smiled. The suggestion of a smile crossed his face, then widened when he saw our poodle beside me. His two front teeth, partially blackened from a fall in Korea, were revealed for the first time.

The newest member of our family came downstairs and ate four bananas, two bowls of rice, and an orange. He gave half his toast to Ivan, the poodle.

Mark had stepped from his world, across the long, hard bridge, into ours.

Chapter 5

Life at our house soon surged with new energy. Within twenty-four hours of Mark's arrival, we were all down on the college playing field. Alex hoped to teach Mark the ins and outs of baseball. He had picked out, with his dad's help, a baseball mitt for his new brother.

For a five-year-old, Mark's throw was amazingly long and accurate. After catching the first ball Alex threw to him, he kept motioning Alex to move farther back on the playing field. Alex flashed happy looks of disbelief at Sarah, Cameron, and me as the distance between the two boys increased. Finally, Mark indicated he was satisfied. He took aim. Gleeful shouts accompanied the delight that broke over our faces as the ball, straight and strong, soared toward Alex. Clearly impressed, Alex whooped out, "Did you see *that*!"

So much was trial and error. We taught ourselves imperfect Korean from a tape and a sheet of "useful phrases." I taped a list of key words on the refrigerator door and upstairs on our bathroom mirror:

hello... *annyong-h*
thank you... *gomapsumnida*
yes... *nye*
no... *aniyo*
brother... *hyong-nim*
sister... *nu-nim*
father... *aboji*
mother... *o-mo-ni*
grandmother... *hal mo-ni*

We all learned to say *sarang-heyo* for "I love you" and *oshipshiyo* meaning "please come." Mark's English consisted of "hello," "goodbye," "thank you," "yes," and "no."

Communicating the *do's* and *don'ts* was a challenge. Our attempts often turned into a comic game of charades. "We do *not* urinate from the second-floor balcony onto the garden below."(*much* to the disappointment of wide-eyed neighborhood children.) "We *do* sit inside the car—*not* on top of it." "We *do* stop our tricycle before zipping into the street."

Mark's adaptability amazed us. After only one night he managed to maneuver his somewhat bewildered brother out of the top bunk bed and claim it as his own. After two days, he let me take off the turtleneck and shorts he'd arrived in and ease his tired, tense body into a warm bath.

Barbara Adams had asked us to send her photographs of Mark within the first two days so she could airmail them to his birth mother. A friend loaned us a Polaroid, and we were able to send many pictures of Mark, safe within his new family.

Mark entered kindergarten within a few days, although there were only three weeks left in the school year. His new classmates squealed with delight each time he repeated an English word or joined in a game. Every afternoon when I picked him up, a child would come up to me and tell me about Mark's day.

"Mark can kick the ball really hard!"

"He likes it when we march around the room."

"Mark made us all laugh. He sure can make funny faces."

Mark relished Korean staples like rice and *kimchi*. New foods, especially spaghetti, ginger cookies, and cheddar cheese became favorite things to eat. And bananas by the bunch disappeared at snack time.

Our animals became a bridge, helping to ease him into his new world. Love was instantaneous and mutual with Ivan, our large poodle, and with Kitten Kaboodle, our affectionate gray cat. With a little more caution, Mark warmed to the brother who had awaited him so eagerly. The brothers' nightly bath together often exploded into noisy, wet scenes. They played with plastic toys, including a small yellow and blue boat that was in the satchel Mark had brought. Fast motors roared through the waves, causing collisions and submersions. Water swooshed and sloshed amid English phrases, Korean expressions, and laughter.

When I read a second story to the boys after their bath (with all three of us settled on the large bed), Mark would always jump down to get his favorite book from the pile. He'd hand me *Chitty-Chitty-Bang-Bang*, repeating the title two or three times, with a smile and a toss of his head.

Mark kept the small satchel and the red toy car he had brought with him by the pillow on his bed. During his second week at our house—after a particularly active day—Cameron and I heard him singing lullabies as he lay on the top bunk. Without his knowing, we captured them on tape.

Several times in the early months he sat quietly in our backyard, his arm around Ivan, looking off into space. I found myself trying to imagine not only what or who he might be thinking about or yearning for but also how this move to a totally new life was affecting this almost six-year-old. I had grown up myself the youngest of five children, in the security of a loving family, living in the same home with happy memories of summers on Cape Cod—and the predictability of following in my siblings' path but on my own terms. What would it have been like for me as a five- or six-year-old to lose all that, I mused. What if my early years had been ones of anxiety, uncertainty, and conflict? I bit my tongue hard. I had no answers. But my heart was able to embrace the scene before me—the large black poodle, the perfect friend, being hugged by his new young friend!

Usually on the move, Mark scampered everywhere, investigating, experimenting, immersing himself in the world about him. One morning he disappeared on his tricycle. I quickly alerted campus security, and then enlisted two women friends who lived nearby to help me look for him. He soon turned up, grinning from ear to ear, seated next to Jack, a security guard. His tricycle sat in back of the two-seat, three-wheeled vehicle used by staff around campus. Jack, a longtime friend, chuckled. "I found him going lickety-split down the steepest hill on campus. His feet were off the pedals, and he was having the time of his life!"

One day not long after that incident, a small bicycle arrived for him, a gift from his New England grandparents. After supper that evening, we took it across the street to a grassy area so he could practice. He climbed on the bicycle and took off. The only problem was that he didn't know how to stop. Cameron, Sarah, Alex, and I flew after him trying to catch hold. The more we chased him, the faster he went. He laughed uproariously, thinking this was some kind of game. Finally, doubled over and exhausted, we plopped down on the grass to watch him gradually slow down and at long last fall gently to the side. A few days later, Alex and I watched him crouch next to his upside-down bicycle and turn the pedals by hand to see how the wheels spun around.

Mark soon became one of the "kids on the block," tagging along, joining in. Craig, a three-year-old neighbor, fell off his tricycle where several children were playing. He wasn't hurt, but he cried hard. Craig's dad came through the backyard, to poke his head in the kitchen door. "I think you should know that your new son left what he was doing with the other boys and went right over to Craig, sat down beside him, and put his arm around him until I got there. When he knew Craig was all right, he went back to the group."

"Thanks for telling me, Ed. Happily, I'm not surprised... maybe because I've been aware of his caring and affection for our animals." Later when I saw Mark I thanked him for helping Craig. He looked at me, shrugged his shoulders and scooted off again.

In June, Mark met his other siblings as our expanded family gathered together for the first time. Timothy came home for a week of army leave from New Mexico. Emily arranged to take her vacation at the same time. Tim had daily wrestling bouts in the back yard with his young brothers. They took turns wearing his army hat and tagged after him whenever they could. Emily and Sarah had them singing and dancing, "crazy-like," said Alex.

"Mark sure seems to be enjoying himself. I'm amazed how well he knows his way around," Tim observed as he, Emily, and I sat out on the porch one afternoon.

"He's so gentle with the animals," Emily added. "Do you think he had a pet in Korea?"

"I doubt it. I think his mother had a struggle getting food for the two of them," I answered.

Emily looked thoughtful. "Boy, it must be hard for him to have all his thoughts in Korean and not be able to share them."

"He and Alex sure have fun together—no trouble communicating there, that's for sure. I wonder when he'll feel comfortable with English," Tim said.

"Maybe by the end of the summer," I said. "According to what I've read, first he'll have to make sense out of what he hears. To internalize it as a very young child does. Then he'll begin to speak English."

"From what I've seen, it won't be long," Emily said. "Oh, here they come." She opened the porch door as Alex and Mark came running toward us.

"Tim," Alex begged, "come shoot baskets with us!" The three brothers manuevered noisily around the driveway hoop until suppertime.

여 섯 *Chapter 6*

Alex and Mark differed in many ways, but—much to our joy—they became good friends. Alex accepted his new brother wholeheartedly from the first. He helped him make countless adjustments to his new life. This did not, however, preclude squabbles, misunderstandings, and occasional rifts. I remember smiling when I first heard their voices raised, shouting at each other in disagreement. I knew then that they were truly brothers!

This, then, was the child we received from afar, or the part of him he let us know. Mark was an affectionate child and when Cameron or I put our arms around him as we said goodbye or at bedtime, he hugged us back willingly. Mark could also slam doors; he wasn't going to be pushed around by anyone. But he had a basic trust in others and in the world. Young Ho had said goodbye to everything and everyone he had ever known. He'd flown off and far away, landing feet first as Mark on the other side of the world.

And he, himself, guided us in many ways. Watching him, Cameron and I learned that he preferred to remain in the neighborhood on Saturday mornings rather than join others of similar backgrounds at the Korean Cultural Center thirty-five miles away. Mark kept in touch with his Asian roots by singing lullabies, listening to records of traditional Korean music played on a twelve-stringed zither (*kayagum*) or mouth organ (*saenghwang*), and by hearing the folktales we read him from an illustrated book, *A Korean Grab Bag*. In his room hung a large copy of a 13th-century brush painting depicting frolicking Korean boys.

In the fall he entered first grade. With the help of a remarkable teacher and a college student who worked alone with him twice a week, Mark made good progress. It would take time to close the gaps, but Kate Leary and Robert Mead recognized his needs and his special gifts. Robert told us he observed Mark often on the playground. "Mark never gets into fights or tangles. He usually walks away if trouble's brewing. He's a different kind of kid."

The following May, on a Tuesday morning after Sarah and Alex left for school and Cameron rode off to campus on his bike, I buckled Mark into the seat behind me and we headed for the Federal Building in St. Paul. Mark was about to become an *American citizen!*

There were ten or twelve adults of various ethnic backgrounds who smiled when Mark, age seven, was seated with them. When at last his turn came, he was asked to repeat certain words given to him by the patient, soft-spoken judge. Then in an exuberant, welcoming voice each was declared a full American Citizen and given a small American flag amidst much clapping among the audience. And I wished every "natural" American citizen could be present at such a deeply moving event.

On our way back to his first-grade class at school that afternoon we stopped at the bakery to pick up the pre-ordered cupcakes, each topped with a tiny American flag. It was a banner day for Mark. He sat center stage and loved it! The children in the class surprised him with a tall Uncle Sam's hat made with the art teacher's help. Mr. Downs, the principal, came in to congratulate him and stayed for cake and lemonade. His classmates clustered around, admiring the certificate he'd been given by the judge in St. Paul that morning. Everyone sang all four verses of *America*, while the teacher pointed to the words written on the board. The weekly newspaper printed a picture of Mark in his hat, beaming and surrounded by his classmates.

A few times in second and third grade Mark came home from school visibly upset—lips taut, eyes somber. I did not try to speak with him right away, and he couldn't (or wouldn't) talk to me. Once he came in the house after tossing his bike on the front lawn, ran upstairs, and slammed the door. I knew something painful had happened and sensed he needed time by himself. After a while I went up to him. His bureau drawers were pulled out, the clothes strewn all over the room. His bookcase had been emptied. He lay face down on the bed, his head buried under his pillow.

I sat on the edge of Mark's bed, stroking his back. Gently I coaxed him to tell me what happened. Two older boys, he finally told me, had run alongside him a few blocks from school, chanting, "Hello, Chink, Chink." They mocked him in singsong tones as he tried to escape from them on his bike, only to have his way blocked. Finally an adult walking by interceded. His chest heaving, Mark burst out, "I want to go back to Korea."

I swallowed my own tears enough to say soothingly, "Oh, that must have hurt a lot. Do you know those boys from school, Mark?"

"Not really," he said.

"Do they have many friends at school?" I asked.

"No! Everyone says they're bullies," Mark said emphatically as he slowly sat up beside me on the edge of his bed. Ivan, who waited for Mark's arrival from school each afternoon, had followed me into the room. He sat on his haunches, never taking his eyes off his distraught friend. Mark put out his hand and the dog wiggled toward him.

I put my arm around Mark. "Those boys probably don't feel very good about themselves. Maybe things don't go well for them at home. Anyway, you were wise to keep on riding and to come right home. I'm so sorry this happened."

I gently took hold of Mark's chin with my other hand, moving his face around so that I could look into his eyes. "About Korea," I said, "we'd miss you terribly, Mark. We couldn't imagine our lives without you."

After a few minutes we came downstairs. "Let's see where Alex is," I said. "Ivan, you come too. We're going to the Dairy Queen!"

Chapter 7

When Mark had been with us two years, a note arrived from our social worker: "We've had word that your son's family is having a difficult time. Please send pictures."

We did—pictures of Mark making angels in the snow, hugging Ivan, playing softball with Cameron and Alex, sitting at his desk at school. For weeks after they were mailed, I wondered if they had reached her. I hoped her yearning for him was eased by seeing his happy grin. Or did the photographs intensify her pain, as they would have for me? I imagined her tears, and the pain in her heart that would not go away.

Often I thought of her. Again I mused: For almost six years she had cared for him, had begun each day by his side, had shared space with him in the darkness. I thought about their years together and the intimate bonding of this mother and her child. The fact that she had kept him until it was time for him to go to school... and then had to face the fact: He could *not* go to school in Korea.

Now it was I, Martha, who was in that relationship with Mark. He was an important part of my life, but the loss his first mother continually faced was deep inside me.

I tried to imagine saying goodbye to Alex—sending him away, forever. Halfway across the world... to Russia or China or Korea. Often in the early morning, I'd lie in that semi-dream state and envision myself in those last moments with my child—stooping down to zip his jacket, looking into his large dark eyes, searching for words. I tried to imagine the aftershock, the guilt, the uncertainty. And worst of all, the finality.

When Timothy and Emily departed recently from home, my sadness was tinged with excitement and pride. They were trying their wings. Sarah, too, would leave for college in the fall. But I knew they could—and would—sometimes fly home.

I wondered if, for the sake, for the love of my child, I could do what Mark's mother had done. I knew how to embrace a child, but I didn't know if I'd have the stamina or courage to let one go.

And what of Young Ho? Had a curtain crashed down, cutting Mark off from his earlier years? Surely, he had some means of glancing back. Still in the midst of his new life did he sometimes feel pain? Or was his past buried too deeply within his psyche? What was concealed in his secret hiding place? Cameron and I did not know, and although we wondered, we did not probe.

Only four times in twelve years did Mark refer directly to his early years in Korea.

We were making preparations for his first Christmas with us. English sentences had already begun to roll miraculously off his tongue. As he pressed the rolling pin back and forth over the cookie dough, he said, without raising his head, "I've done this before, with my grandmother."

"Did you cut the cookies out and decorate them?"

Mark shrugged his shoulders. Was he too intrigued with the task at hand to continue? Or perhaps this memory that bubbled to the surface surprised him, catching him painfully off guard.

Not long afterward, he caught sight of lobsters in a tank at a fish market. He jumped up and down excitedly, "I caught one once, down by the river. I caught it with my hands and ran home with it! I remember my grandmother put it in a big black pot, and we ate it."

During a sabbatical year when Mark was eight, we traveled one day by train in Indonesia through the countryside dotted with rice fields. At one point Mark leaned forward in his seat.

"See those reeds over there? I used to gather those and weave them together."

"What did you make?" Alex asked.

"I don't remember."

Except for these fragments, Mark's early years seemed out of reach, inaccessible, somewhere behind a curtain. Other pieces or whole patterns from his early years may have come into his consciousness, but were pushed back.

About a year after he came into our family, Mark was splashing in the tub with his brother Alex. "I never had a mother," Mark told him. "Only my grandmother and an older sister. Sometimes I went and spent weekends with my sister."

We knew Mark had, since the age of three, lived part of the time with his grandmother. We also knew that he must have felt close to her.

Across the street from our house, in a second-floor apartment, lived an eighty-year-old, white-haired woman we called Granny. Soon after he came, Mark ran across the street when he saw her out walking, using a cane. He stood on the grass by the sidewalk as her large bent frame came close to him. Her gentle eyes met his as he looked up at her. Granny stooped down, spoke to him and gathered him close to her. Did she remind him of his own grandmother? After that, he ran to her whenever he saw her, showing her something from his pocket, bringing her a flower from the garden—and each time he was hugged.

We surmised that his "older sister" was, in fact, his mother. Perhaps, for Mark's sake, she referred to herself in this way as a step toward letting him go. Perhaps thinking of herself as an older sibling to Young Ho, rather than as his mother, would make the coming separation less painful. Maybe, knowing already what she must decide for him, she was trying to ease her child—and herself—into the separation.

In January of 1979, when Mark was fourteen, Cameron and I were having coffee at the breakfast table and reading the Saturday paper. Alex had already left for hockey practice at the high school rink. We heard Mark rumbling around in his room above the kitchen. In a few minutes he came down, not quite awake, in his hockey gear. While he was eating his second bowl of Raisin Bran, he looked across the table at me and said, "Do you know where in Korea I was born?"

"I can't remember, but I think it was outside of Seoul," I said, trying not to reveal astonishment in my voice. "I have it in your folder upstairs. Do you want me to get it?"

"Sure!" he answered. "Just thinking about a short story we read in English class yesterday. This middle-aged man doesn't know where he was born or anything about his early life before he became an orphan. I started thinking—I don't know any of that either."

I returned with the folder he hadn't wanted to look at a few years earlier. I sat at the table next to him as he opened up the *Adoptive Child Study Summary* and found the heading *Place of birth*. I struggled to read the name of the place. "Daejon-Ni, Chongsan-Myon, Pochon-Kun, Kyonggi-Do, Korea."

Cameron looked up from the paper. "It sounds as though you were born in three or four places!"

"Sure, Dad! Didn't I tell you? I'll have to get out the map of Korea and see where that is." Mark picked up the report and read the short paragraphs quickly, flipping through five pages. He pushed back his chair and changed the subject. "Mom, how's about a ride to the rink? Mr. Johnson hates it when we're late."

As we drove to the high school, I said, "Shall I put the folder in your room so you can look at it again?"

"Yeah, sure."

"Dad and I will be glad to talk with you, if you have any questions," I offered.

"OK, thanks…", and climbing out of the car with his hockey gear, "and for the ride, too."

We didn't hear any more about Korea until a few years later when Cameron and I told the boys that he and I planned to spend a year in Japan. Cameron would be directing and teaching in an undergraduate program in a school, based in Kyoto, Japan's ancient capital, that drew students from twelve liberal-arts colleges across the United States. Mark unexpectedly said, "I'd like to spend some time in Japan with you." Then he added: "I'd like to go to Korea, too."

"That's great," I said, surprised and delighted "Let's do it! The summer before the program begins we'll have some time."

A familiar thought began to haunt me then—one that had been with me since the night of Mark's first plane ride across the planet. Mark's birth mother was still a presence in my life, however shadowy. I still felt her remorse and yearning and my heart ached for her.

One beautiful Sunday afternoon in October 1982, nine months before our departure for the Orient, Cameron and I walked with Ivan along the river path. As we ambled along, I posed the question that had been on my mind for years. "Cameron, do you think Mark has ever thought about finding his birth mother? When we visit Korea maybe he'd like to see her again. Maybe he's dealing with unresolved feelings of abandonment."

Cameron answered thoughtfully. "No doubt, it's lurking there somewhere inside him. I've been thinking about this, too. A young child like Mark who spent his early years with one family and then had that relationship severed, without understanding why, must have many questions, even when there's been a good adjustment to a new environment.

"Maybe, that's why he wants to come with us. I've tried to imagine how much Mark understood when he said goodbye to his birth mother. Maybe all he was able to grasp at the time was the excitement of flying off on an enormous jet. Sometime in the last twelve years, the awesome truth must have dawned on him—"when I was five years and ten months old, my mother sent me away."

"Remember when he first looked at his folder? I'm not sure he could identify himself as the little boy he read about, or the picture pasted on the first sheet. He even said, 'That doesn't look like me!'"

Cameron kicked a stick out of the way. "We told him about the problems he would have had in Korea as a racially mixed child. Maybe that helped some in his understanding why his mother sent him here. But I've always felt sad that he is cut off from those early important years of his life."

"I feel a deep bond with Mark's birth mother," I told him. "It's been there from the first. I know so little about her, and yet I feel close to her—in part, because I feel the gnawing ache she must have inside her. She gave him such a nurturing, sustaining kind of love. I'm sure that's a large part of why he's made such a good adjustment here."

Cameron smiled. "Don't forget what our social worker said… we might have had something to do with that."

"Yes, I remember, but Barbara agrees with me. She thinks Mark must have had very special love growing up."

The following afternoon when I came home from my half-time teaching job, I called the adoption agency in Minneapolis. It had been nine years since we were in touch with Barbara Adams and she no longer worked there. I asked to speak with someone who had helped adopted children get in touch with their birth families in Korea. When Mr. Larson came on the phone, I told him of our plans to visit Korea.

"For several years, my husband and I have wished that someday our son could accept those early years and recognize them as part of who he is and is becoming. He left Korea when he was too young to understand what was happening to him. Perhaps when he first got here he just couldn't look back. Maybe that was the only way he could cope—by immersing himself in the present."

Mr. Larson was a good listener, so I kept talking. "As Mark grew, we saw signs that his thoughts sometimes turned to the Orient. Although these seem small things, he never missed "Kung Fu" on TV. Recently he's been reading articles on Eastern forms of meditation and karate. We were so glad he asked about coming to Japan with us, and possibly visiting Seoul. In fact, Cameron and I have a sense that unless Mark reconnects in some way with his life in Korea, he'll carry around unanswered questions all his life."

Mr. Larson waited until I finished. Then he spoke from decades of experience with adoptions. He talked about the healing that can come to the child and to the mother from resolving feelings of abandonment and guilt. "It allows both to find a sense of wholeness," he said.

"We don't know for sure, but we assume that Mark received a lot of love early in life," I told Mr. Larson. "Someone instilled in him a wonderful sense of trust. We want him to understand that his mother's and grandmother's deep love gave them the courage to send him away. We want him, through understanding and love, to forgive and let go."

"If anything," Mr. Larson said, "for the mother, the sense of guilt at having 'abandoned' the child is probably deeper, more intense than the wound felt by the child."

"I can imagine that she carries it in her heart and mind at all times," I said, "even if she is aware that he is happy and thriving in his new life. Mr. Larson, I need to tell you that for years I have had visions of this woman—Mark's birth mother."

Mr. Larson said softly, "I understand." He encouraged us to continue, but carefully. "Sometimes," he said, "premature contact with a birth family can complicate long-festering wounds. It is particularly tricky where unresolved questions lurk." He also told me that the adoption agency could do nothing to activate a birth-parent search until Mark expressed his own desire in writing.

"I wonder if it would ease the pain," I said to Cameron later that night, "if Mark's birth mother knew how he is now, what kind of a person he is? I think—No, I *know*... if I had sent a child away and mourned that loss but somehow learned he was doing well... yes, it would bring comfort. No doubt about that!"

In the autumn preceding our summer departure for the Far East, we drove Mark to some college interviews. He was going to be a freshman the following fall. On one of these trips, Mark sat up front with his dad. I leaned forward from the back seat and took a deep breath. At least this way, moving along the highway at night, his first reactions to the possibility of finding his birth mother would remain his own. I did not want him to answer quickly. And I didn't want to make it difficult for him—or me—by speaking face to face.

"Mark, have you ever thought that you might want to locate your birth mother in Korea?" I asked.

In the darkness, he wrapped his silence with the slight shift of his body and a barely perceptible hunch of his shoulders.

Cameron added quietly, "We've been wondering because of our trip next summer. But, don't give us your answer now. Think about it carefully and let us know."

"It will be your decision, Mark," I added.

Mark gave no indication of his feelings that night, or in the weeks to come.

A month later, I sat sipping coffee at the supper table while Mark was working on his second dessert. His brother Alex had called from college while we were eating to say he'd be home the next weekend. Cameron had gone upstairs to get ready for a faculty meeting. Mark and I watched a squirrel trying to raid the birdfeeder just outside the bay window. I got up and began to wash dishes at the sink. Suddenly I asked Mark, in a deliberately casual way, if he had come to any decision. I turned to see his reaction.

He looked directly at me and said softly, "I need more time." Then he added, "Part of me wants to visit Korea and have some sense of my roots there—and let it go at that. But there is part of me that wants the other, too."

"It's an important decision," I said. "Why don't you put down in writing the pros and cons?"

The next day Mark showed us his list. In the "con" column, he had written:

> I don't know her.
>
> My life is so different now and I feel like an American.
>
> How would I communicate, what would I say?

It could be uncomfortable, painful.

And in the other column:

I'm curious about my past.

I might not get to Korea again for a long time, if ever.

Would things look familiar?

I wonder what she's like.

I wonder if I'd recognize her.

Then he said quietly, "It really comes down to curiosity. I'll write the letter even though I still feel ambivalent. But, yes, basically I want to do it."

여덟 *Chapter 8*

In the northern outskirts of Seoul, we were scheduled to visit the Korean adoption agency where our son had spent some time before coming to us. Cameron telephoned to get directions. They had been waiting for our call. A car would pick us up the next morning for the hour-long ride, they told him. And they had been unable to locate Mark's birth mother, though they would continue the search.

Mark was stretched out on a bed in the hotel room, staring up at the ceiling and listening to his dad talking on the phone. When Cameron repeated to us what he'd been told, Mark turned silently toward the wall. Later he joined us for a simple meal in the hotel restaurant, but he was unnaturally quiet. He chose to return upstairs to our room rather than accompany us on our nightly stroll. When we returned from our walk, he was either asleep, or pretending to be.

I lay awake thinking about the last few days—the ferry ride, the long bus ride through the countryside and villages, the restaurant scene, the time with Professor Kim and his family. Mark had enjoyed art treasures and culinary delights. He'd read every English pamphlet he could get his hands on.

"Did you know that centuries ago Koreans heated their houses by running pipes under their floors?" he had asked excitedly. "And their phonetic system is supposed to be one of the most efficient in the world!"

And, tomorrow... what would it bring? Tomorrow at the orphanage Mark would come closer to his first six years of life. Thoughts of what it might bring kept me tossing and turning… if my mind and heart were filled with such turbulence, what must Mark be experiencing? Tomorrow he would come face to face with memories that had been bottled up for fourteen years.

Emotionally exhausted, I finally fell asleep, only to be awakened by a bad dream. In the dream, I awoke in our hotel room to find Mark's bed empty. He had disappeared and had taken only his small sports bag with him. I ran to the window and saw Mark walking away, and a shadowy figure at his side. Jolted awake, I sat up terrified and perspiring. I fell back on the pillow, saying a prayer of gratitude. For I could almost reach out and touch my son's body as he lay on the rollaway cot across the small room. His chest rose and fell in slow, rhythmic breathing. Deep down, did I, myself, harbor the fear of losing Mark?

I wondered if we had made a mistake in bringing him back.

As I lay there trying to recover, hoping sleep would overtake me, I thought of the Noh theatre performance we had seen with Mark when we first got to Japan earlier in the summer. It was called *Sakuragawa* ('Cherry River'), and was written in the 14th century. It concerns a mother whose son sells himself into slavery to provide her with much-needed funds. Her frenzied longing for her child drives her insane, and she wanders aimlessly from her home to find him. When at last the woman is reunited with her child, they enter a monastery together.

My heart was filled with sadness for all those who lose a child. And for those who fear they might.

The car arrived from the agency early the next morning. We jerked along in the teeming traffic until we reached the outskirts of the city and began to move at a steady pace. A range of mountains rose in the west. The rice fields, farm houses, gardens, and clusters of simple wooden dwellings presented a refreshing change from Seoul.

Mark, silent and tense, sat up front with the driver. Again and again, I saw the muscles of his jaw tighten. Eventually we made an abrupt turn onto a narrow road that curved past a few small utility sheds. A group of low buildings surrounded a playground. As an open space came into view, the driver gave two short toots on the horn.

Immediately, the entire office staff of four or five people poured out of the building to greet us. One of the men opened the door on Mark's side, and our son was the first out of the car. As soon as Mark had both feet on the ground, Mr. Pak, the former director, moved toward him. Mark stood straight and stiff—uncertain, perhaps fearful—just as he had when we first met him at the airport. Mr. Pak's bulky frame was clad in casual trousers and a bright, cool shirt open at the neck. Their eyes met, then Mr. Pak stepped up to him and enfolded him in his arms. He held him close, saying over and over in his distinct clear accent, "Welcome, my boy, welcome."

Mrs. C., a secretary, clasped her hands together, bit her lip, and then laughed. Surprised by the joyful mood, our tight-lipped son visibly relaxed and even broke into a grin. His arms, which at first had remained stiffly by his side, moved upward and around his greeter's ample girth.

The warm welcome we enjoyed at the adoption center set a relaxed stage for our visit. Everyone was kind and generous in talking with us, some in broken, others in fluent English. Whatever fears or uncertainties Mark had about coming appeared to melt away. Mr. Pak was outspoken in his delight that one of "his children" had returned. Yes, he remembered our son well!

"You were very good about helping with the younger children. You comforted them when they needed it," Mr. Pak said. I told him how Mark, soon after he had come to us, had gone to help a little neighborhood boy who was hurt. Mr. Pak nodded and turned to Mark. "And, oh, how you could hit that ball just right during kick ball," he said, giving his stocky leg an energetic thrust forward.

"We were astounded at how far he could throw a ball when he first came to us," Cameron said.

Mr. Pak put his hand on Mark's shoulder, "Yes, I remember that, too."

Mark grinned, then said, pointing, "I remember, I think, a big shed or some building on the far side of the playground."

Mr. Pak smiled. "Over there, that building must be the one. When you were only this high," he moved his outstretched hand toward the ground, "that shed *did* tower over you."

We laughed and followed him into the main building. While sipping tea in his office, he told us about the social service agency and Korea's taboo on the adoption of unrelated persons.

"None of the babies you'll see when I take you to the nursery were born here. The infants are brought to us. Very few are adopted into Korean families, because of the stigma of having an *outside* child. Family lineage is almost sacred."

"What if couples cannot have children?" I asked.

"Sometimes adoptions take place within the extended family." Mr. Pak answered, putting his round teacup in front of him and leaning forward on his elbows. He looked intently at us with deep-set eyes. "But it can be heart-rending. Just last week a man and his wife came here. At first glance, the woman looked very pregnant. But they said they wanted to adopt a baby. I looked at the woman and said kindly, 'Why don't you take the pillow out? You'll be more comfortable.'

"Then the couple told me that the doctors said they would not be able to have children. They were deeply saddened, but then decided on a plan. The wife added to her girth a little each month until close to the 'birth' time. Then she left her village neighborhood, saying she was going 'back home' to be with her mother for the birth of the child, still a common custom in Korea. When they returned home, the child they adopted would be welcomed and loved by the neighbors—who had no reason to suspect it wasn't a child born to them." He paused, and then happily added, "They went home with a beautiful baby boy!"

Mr. Pak told us about efforts to locate Mark's birth mother. They had gone to the neighborhood of the last address they had. "It was in Ulsan, a middle-sized city. But thirteen years is a long time," he said quietly, "and no one there who remembered her knew where she was."

Looking at Mark, he went on, "We do have a few more leads and we'll keep trying." Mark, whose eyes dropped when Mr. Pak started talking about his mother, responded to the last remark with a nod to Mr. Pak and a glance toward his parents. I clung hopefully to his words "we do have a few more leads" and could not let them go.

We toured the facilities, walking past dozens of clotheslines where hundreds of brightly colored diapers fluttered in the sun. Red, blue, green, and yellow diapers danced merrily on the line, looking almost like Tibetan prayer flags!

We entered a two-story building that housed three separate nurseries and a small infirmary. Everything looked immaculate. Mr. Pak told us that six nurses and six aides cared for the seventy-plus children, who were divided according to age or need. Some of the nurses, he told us, had been there many years. They seemed delighted to see us—and especially to see Mark.

We looked around, amazed. Korean and Amer-Asian babies, several almost newborn, but most two or three months old, lay in bassinets or in cribs. A few looked as old as seven or eight months. Black hair, beautiful skin, waving arms, moving legs. Some smiled at us, a few cried. Most had just been fed.

"Each baby is held by one of these good people when given its bottle," Mr. Pak told us. He gestured to a corner where two young aides in rocking chairs fed the tiny infants cradled in their arms. "Most of the children are here for only a few months, awaiting adoption either in America or Europe." Mark touched the hand of a little girl held by a nurse. The six-month-old baby curled her fingers around Mark's and held on tight. "Ouch!" he feigned, and the baby laughed.

We next walked past the playground with its swings and jungle gym to a low building where we heard children chattering inside. The door opened, and a dozen pairs of dark eyes looked up at us from the floor. There the children squatted, playing a game with a young woman.

These three-, four-, and five-year-olds were waiting for families to adopt them. In a friendly voice, in Korean, Mr. Pak told the children that the tall boy by his side had slept in this very room when he was their size. "Now he lives in America," he added in English. Several of them got up and came over to him. "Hell-o," one of the boys ventured, grinning self-consciously. Soon the others joined in, giggling. Totally at ease, Mark responded to them warmly, shaking hands and patting black-topped heads.

By mid-morning, I felt the deep, quiet joy of knowing that something good was taking place. We were all making the first real connection with Mark's past. And Mark was leading the way.

Mr. Pak took the three of us halfway up the mountain in his car for a feast of Korean dishes. His merriment was infectious. Toward the end of the meal, he told Mark that he was very good at arranging marriages. "Please, just let me know if you're interested!"

Surprised, Mark looked at Mr. Pak, lowered his eyes, and muttered with a smile and a shake of his head, "No, thanks!"

Mr. Pak thanked us again and again for coming, saying it had been an important and wonderful day for him. "You are a fine young man, Mark," he added. "Please always think of this place as one of your homes. You are welcome here, any time."

It was time to go and we departed, reluctantly, not wanting the warmth and kindness of this place, this day to pass. The office staff came out to bid us goodbye. "Please come back!" they shouted. "Thank you for coming and good luck!" As we drove off, Mr. Pak waved to us with the hand that held an envelope of photographs of Mark and our family—just in case his mother was found.

Mark was very quiet for the rest of the day and went to bed early. That night I wrote in my journal:

"One of the happier days of my life! A few key pieces of the puzzle are in place. I think something very basic took place today for Mark. Like turning around and seeing for the first time where he'd come from. Being able to say, 'I remember being here.' He'd stepped off the bridge to the other side and come face to face with his past. I was a mother, watching, warmed by mysterious forces at work. I'm glad, somehow, that Mark didn't meet his birth mother today. I think he needs more time. That's true for me, too. Nothing, I think, could have helped Mark as much as this wonderful day with Mr. Pak."

Mark said very little as we were driven back to our hotel in Seoul. He got into bed early and closed his eyes.

아 흑 *Chapter 9*

We left Seoul the next day by bus, heading for the east coast and a mountainous area. After Seoul, the lofty peaks and ocean view were welcome sights. The three of us descended Mt. Sorak by cable car, looking down on the sloping temple roofs barely visible in the forested valley below, and walked the mile or so back to our hotel along a wide footpath. Clumps of brightly colored wildflowers grew along the way. A mountain stream rushed past, rolling and turning its way to the sea. Our faces were sun flushed from hours on the rocks above. We exchanged only a few words.

As my thoughts turned to a cold drink and resting my feet, an extraordinary thing happened. Mark began to remember.

"I don't think we lived in Seoul. There were lots of rice fields. It was a tiny village with only one store. I slept on the floor. One night I woke up and saw a man with one of those funny, broad rimmed hats on. He was digging outside my room and I watched him carefully because I didn't know what he was doing. There was an army base on top of a nearby hill; I used to go there in my bare feet."

Cameron and I exchanged a quick glance as Mark spoke, moving along between us, his eyes on the path ahead. We dared not interrupt. I think I stopped breathing.

"I remember once being brought to a place, maybe I was sick ... there was a knock on the door and someone bowed when it was opened. Maybe it was a temple or the doctor's. There was only one girl in the village; all the others were boys. I had a toy boat, like a steamship.

Someone gave it to me. It whistled. I used to put it in a well in the courtyard and play with it. I remember the adoption center where we were yesterday. I was looking for a big barn with a tin roof. I slept on the floor in that big room and I remember playing on the playground. I remember Mr. Pak, too, and the little bump on the side of his cheek. Once a car came and I was asked whether I wanted to go to my sister's or my grandmother's. I didn't know what was going on."

Bits and pieces, tinged with pleasure, pain, and uncertainty broke the seal of silence. More would surface now, I knew, even if Mark did not tell us.

Cameron's eyes met mine. He put his arm around Mark's shoulder. I touched Mark's arm. We walked in silence the rest of the way to our hotel, but I felt I could have climbed right up the side of Mount Sorak! When we got back to our hotel, I quietly went to the desk and wrote down what we had just heard.

The next day there was another long bus trip down the east coast. A two-day stopover at Kwong-ju, the ancient capital, was followed by a stop in Pusan, where we would catch the ferry back to Japan. In Pusan we scurried in and out of several shops to locate the one thing Mark wanted to buy—a large Korean flag to hang in his room at college.

In August 1983, Mark left us to begin college in northern Wisconsin. Cameron and I settled into life in Kyoto for the school year. In October, we had a note from the adoption agency in Minnesota. They had received word from Seoul that an uncle of Mark's was living in Pusan. The uncle indicated that his sister, Mark's birth mother, lived in a suburb of Pusan. She was married to an American serving in the armed forces. The note said we should feel free to write to the uncle. We could mail our letter to the agency in Minneapolis, and they would translate our letter and send it back to Pusan. I could barely contain my excitement.

I wrote to Mark to let him know that an uncle had been located. We wrote the same to Tim, Emily, Sarah, and Alex in our next letters to them. The next time we heard from them, they, too, were excited by the news. From Mark we heard nothing.

I wanted to tell Mark that his birth mother had been located, but I didn't. Right or wrong, I wanted someone close to him to be there when he received the news. Also, we did not yet know how his birth mother felt about contacting him, or us, and we knew that she had the right to decline.

I wrote to Mark's uncle and explained who we were, and why I was writing. We hoped he and his family had seen the pictures we had left with Mr. Pak.

"We want you and his mother to know that Young Ho has been an important member of our family. He is a fine person and has brought us much happiness. If you or his mother would like to write (and perhaps send a photograph) we would be happy to hear from you. If his mother feels she cannot write, we will understand. Young Ho wondered, too, about his grandmother—if she is alive and well."

Three months passed. We heard nothing. I tried not to think about what that might mean.

Cameron and I found life in Kyoto interesting and very busy. One day in mid-January, after the gala Japanese New Year's celebrations, I was returning from my day at Doshisha University in Kyoto, where I was studying Japanese history, culture, and language.

I glanced at my watch as Bus No. 5 approached our stop in Iwakura, a northern suburb of Kyoto. It was almost four o'clock and already the light of the winter sky had begun to fade. I alighted by the now-dormant rice field just off the busy street, stopped at the convenience store to pick up some milk, and headed for the small house we had called home for the last eight months. The damp cold hit my face and I pulled up the hood of my down coat.

I had welcomed the focus and stimulation of hours of study. It helped me forget that I was half a world away from our children and my ailing parents.

But now I was eager to get back to our house in Iwakura. My head ached and I felt tension in my shoulders—the predictable result of an afternoon spent studying Japanese. I moved along the narrow lanes between the low-tiled roofs and the tiny garden entries of the neighboring homes.

Would there be some mail? A letter from a child, family member, or friend, whose words I could savor over a cup of tea. As I approached our sliding wooden gate, I could see that there was something in the box attached to the post. I lifted out the long white envelope and read the return name and address.

My heartbeat quickened. In the upper right-hand corner was an APO military address underneath the name, Nam Mee Gibson. The letter was from our son's mother.

Across the envelope, written in English, were the words "Do not bend, photographs enclosed." Quickly I moved inside, kicked off my shoes at the entryway, and fumbled into my house slippers. I sank into the small kitchen chair by the table. I put the envelope down. I picked it up. I turned it over. I studied the script. I got up and fixed a cup of tea. I sat down. I held the cup with both hands, sipping the tea in minute portions. My whole being was focused on the unopened envelope now propped before me.

I swallowed hard and carefully pulled off the Scotch tape that secured the flap. As I removed the folded letter, three snapshots slid onto the table. The first was of an older woman seated on the floor behind a low table. Three young boys gathered round her. Across the back of the picture was written: "This is Young Ho's grandmother (she died two years ago) and his cousins, my brother's sons." Their names were given.

In the next picture, one of the cousins—dressed in a school uniform—stood by his father, the man we had written to.

The third photograph was of Mark's birth mother. For years, from the very first days of Mark's arrival, I had visions of the woman who had birthed him, who had said goodbye to him... forever. She had appeared often to me as a shadowy figure—and now for the first time I would see her... distinctly! On the back of the photograph she had printed: "This is me, taken last year." I looked at it feeling deep emotion. I brought it close, wanting to see her face more clearly. Tears came as I held the photo in both hands, reluctant to put it down. Her smile and her dark eyes had such warmth. They were beautiful, like Mark's. High cheek bones gave her face strength and a distinct femininity.

My shoulders hunched up and then relaxed. I let out a deep sigh. This woman, this vague someone I had held strangely close for fourteen years, was now real to me. I could think of her as a particular woman with a lovely face. This was Nam Mee.

Written with the help of a friend, the letter was typewritten and in English. It was a warm and loving response to our overture. She expressed thankfulness in several different ways for the love and care her son had received. She hoped for his continued growth. The letter also revealed some of the pain she carried.

"I got married shortly after Mark was taken up by you. The man was working at the same place as I was, an American service member. His name is Edward Gibson. He had the chance of seeing Mark when he was young. Although it is about 14 years since I got married, we have had no child. I simply didn't want to have any more child as I felt so strongly responsible for what I did to my son, and I decided not to make any more of mine unhappy. I do hope and pray that you will be understanding and tell Mark in a way he can understand. I needed someone to rely upon and comfort me at the time because the fact that I had to send Mark to a strange land was a great shocking to me. It will go without saying but please take care of him as you have done and please ask him to study hard to be a fine citizen. Please take care of yourselves and God bless you and protect you for all time."

I read her words over and over again.

I soon wrote to her again expressing gratitude for her letter and the hope that we could meet. My letter crossed in the mail with a brief letter from her. She, too, wanted to see us before we returned to Minnesota. Her letter also said:

> "Please ask Mark to write to me personally. I do hope he will not bear hard feelings against me but will be understanding."

I replied:

> "I have written to Mark at his college and told him we have heard from you and that you would like to hear from him. It may be difficult for him to write you right away mostly because he will be unsure of what to say. I think it will help him to know that we have been in touch with you. I believe he will want to be in touch with you, but it may take him a while to realize fully that you have been 'found.'"

We did not hear from Mark in response to my letter. That did not surprise us.

Because we had both expressed interest in meeting, in her next letter Nam Mee said she would fly by military pass to Japan, go to her sister's in Nagoya, and travel with her to Kyoto by train. She would arrive in two weeks.

We had no car, but wrote that we could meet them at Lawson's, the convenience store a few minutes walk from our house. The chance of missing them at the large railroad station was too great, and we were uncertain about exactly which train they would be coming on. We asked her to call us from the railway station before they boarded the bus.

Early on the morning of our expected meeting, I woke up feeling as if something wasn't quite real. Fourteen years before, almost to the day, I had that same sensation waiting to meet Mark for the first time. Now it was his mother we were waiting for. I could only nibble at my breakfast. I read the *Japan Times*, as usual, but couldn't remember a word I read. Late that morning, the phone rang. Cameron answered, looking at me as he talked. "Yes, we'll be right there!" he said into the telephone in English.

The call had come not from the train station, but from the store, five minutes away. Nam Mee and her sister had taken a taxi from the station. At that moment they were practically at our doorstep. I gulped, glanced at the tray I had set with teacups, and combed my hair. By the front door, we slid out of our Japanese slippers and into our shoes. We hugged one another quickly and started off, side by side.

We passed our neighbor, Moriyama-san, working his garden.

Konichiwa.

Konichiwa.

Cameron touched my shoulder, saying as we moved along, "How do you think we'd explain to Moriyama-san that we're going to the bus stop to meet our son's mother?" We laughed and I suddenly felt better.

Standing outside the convenience store were two Korean women whose eyes were fixed on us as we crossed the highway. I made a slight waving gesture as we crossed, and suddenly we stood before them. At first I wasn't sure which was Nam Mee and which was her sister. I felt a bit like a shy young girl, not quite sure of myself. I didn't want to offend them in any way by being too open in my gestures or emotions. We smiled and introduced ourselves. Then the younger of the two women, with a slight bow of her head, spoke in a soft voice with a distinct accent. "Hello, I am Nam Mee. And this is my sister, Kaiomi." Nam Mee's eyes filled with tears. I choked back mine, reached out and took her hands in mine. "We are so happy you have come!"

There was a quiet gentleness about Nam Mee as she spoke and interpreted our words for her sister. She had dressed with care in a tan skirt and flowered blouse with a simply styled white jacket. She wore small gold earrings, and her shoulder-length hair was brushed back softly from her high cheekbones. She shared many family traits with her older sister, including the eyes I knew so well. We walked the short distance, through narrow winding streets back to our house, chatting about their trip and what a pleasant day it was.

What took place in our small living room that morning was a miracle. These four people on cushions around a low coffee table had come from opposite sides of the world. Closing gaps of time and space, they drew together out of love for a child who, at the moment, was half a world away.

Nam Mee's English, though simple and at times hesitant, enabled her to tell us some things about herself. She had been born in Japan (when many Koreans were forced to live there to provide cheap labor), but the family had returned to Korea. Recently Nam Mee had spent six months in Arizona and longer periods in Germany and Great Britain, where her husband had been stationed. She told us of her present part-time work as a cashier in a restaurant near the U.S. Air Force base outside of Pusan.

She then withdrew from a large envelope the dozen or so faded and fingered pictures she had brought with her and arranged them carefully in front of us on the table. They were of our son, hers and ours, from infancy up to the age of five years and ten months! We were delighted! It was our first close look at him in those early years. We raised each photo to examine it carefully as she told us when and where each had been taken. "This was when Mark and I lived near Ulsan," she said, handing us a close-up of Mark sitting on a rock. "He was about two then," she added.

"That was his favorite hat his grandmother made for him," Nam Mee told us as she handed us another photo. She explained that Mark sometimes wore the blue wool cap with earflaps to bed in the winter to keep warm. We placed next to those early photos several we had taken over the past dozen years. They documented Mark's progressing in size each year: blowing out birthday candles when he turned seven, showing off his tall Uncle Sam's hat when he became a U.S. citizen, acting silly with his friends, opening his stocking Christmas morning, playing his violin, throwing a football to his brother, and chasing a hockey puck around the ice. We showed her the pictures of Mark and Alex in their British schoolboy uniforms.

"England! When were you there?" she asked excitedly.

"In 1972 and 73, in a place called Onslow Gardens in Muswell Hill, in the north of London."

Nam Mee covered her face with her hands. "You won't believe this! We were at the American Air Force base not far from London the very next year, 1974." And when she saw the picture of Mark standing on the prow of the ferry in Pusan the summer before, Nam Mee burst out, "The U.S. base where we live is twenty minutes away from that harbor!"

Nam Mee picked up the photo of Mark in cap and gown for his high-school graduation. She held it to her bosom, saying, "He looks so grown up."

"I just can't believe he has finished high school and now he's at college!" The photographs of Young Ho—Nam Mee's son—led to the photographs of his young manhood as Mark—our son. Nam Mee's eyes filled with tears and her sister, sitting next to her put her arm around her. "Yes, it is wonderful," I said.

Nam Mee reached again for a picture of the two brothers.

"They both have the same dark brown hair, and Alex looks—like a fun-maker." She wanted to know more about Alex, saying that she had always dreamed and hoped her son would grow up with a brother. Then she placed a large parcel, wrapped in brown paper, on the table. "The gifts in here are for Mark and Alex to share." She opened the bag and showed us half a dozen T-shirts, some striped, all in bright colors.

"Great," I said, "The boys will love them!"

Watching her face, I felt there was more she wanted to tell us. Although we had only met a few hours ago, we felt strangely close. I told her how often I thought of her, wondering about her life and how she was.

"I thought of you, too, without knowing who you were."

Nam Mee leaned forward, resting her arms on the table. Her voice was filled with emotion: "I've felt so much pain for so long because of the decision I had to make for Mark. Sometimes I have not wanted to continue my life. I can't talk about it now. It's just too much all at once."

But, she continued. She spoke of Mark's biological father—and of his returning to the United States without meeting his child. He had been sent to Vietnam, she'd heard, where he had died.

She also told us, in halting tones, what we already knew. A child born of such a union was doomed to shattering pain in South Korea. Nam Mee had been ostracized by family and by neighbors. She turned and looked at her sister. "She was the only family member I could turn to," she said, "though later when my mother was widowed, she helped me care for my son."

Then Nam Mee spoke of the pain she had felt, the pain that was so deep I had felt it on the other side of the planet. Her alert and curious son she said was often tormented by others' cruelty. He would come into the small place where they lived and collapse in a heap on the floor—unable to speak through sobs that wouldn't stop. "Once I got mad at him when he came home crying. 'Why didn't you hit them back?' I asked him. His eyes, swollen with tears, looked up at me and he said, 'Why would I want to do that?'"

The jeers and taunts persisted. He was different, he didn't belong, he was an outsider. She had held him, telling him he was good, not bad, that he must not cry but be strong, that she loved him.

Eventually, although with a broken heart, Nam Mee had to face the reality of his situation. She realized she had to give Young Ho up, to send him to a place and a family where his future would be brighter. In those terrible days, when she often thought of taking both their lives, her agonizing decision was made but the pain never left her. In her heart and soul she knew what she must decide for him. Yet she feared also the pain of knowing he might never understand. She knew that someday he would feel the force of the abandonment and she carried the dreadful fear he would never forgive her. The separation from him then would be complete.

When she had finished, we sat in silence, feeling her agony.

"I'm sorry," she said, "I didn't mean to be so sad."

"We're glad you could tell us, Nam Mee," I said.

Cameron lightened us up, saying, "Nam Mee, Martha and I have wondered how you found out that we were looking for you?"

Nam Mee lowered her eyes as she told us. "When we were stationed in Pusan I went to see a friend in Ulsan, forty-five miles up the coast. Young Ho and I had lived there for several months before I took him to Seoul.

"My friend and I were walking through the village marketplace when someone called my name. It was a woman I knew when I lived in Ulsan. She blurted out excitedly, 'Did they find you? Did they get in touch with you, Nam Mee?'

"I didn't know what she meant. She told me that last summer a man and a woman had come to Ulsan from Seoul and had asked several people at the open market if anyone knew where I lived. This friend told us to go see Sohui, an old friend, who had talked with the two looking for me. My heart began to pound because I thought it might be something about Young-Ho. My friend and I went to Sohui's small house nearby, and she told us that the man and woman were from the adoption agency and they had news about Young Ho."

Nam Mee looked up at us. "I felt faint because—because I thought something terrible had happened to him. Then Sohui smiled at me and told me that you—his American family—wanted to be in touch with me. Sohui had told the people from Seoul that I had a brother who worked for the municipal government in Pusan, and gave them his name.

"I sank down on Sohui's tatami mat and covered my face. My friend was beside me with her arm wrapped about my shoulders. The women were very kind and tried to comfort me and be glad with me at the same time. I'll never forget how I felt. Even as I tell you about it now those feelings of fright and disbelief come back to me.

"When I got back to Pusan the next day, I got in touch with the agency in Seoul. They told me you had been there during the summer. In a few days, I had a letter from my brother enclosing the letter you had sent to him. Then I wrote to you."

When she finished, Nam Mee reached in her purse for a tissue. Numbed, I sat motionless, trying to picture myself, or any mother, in her place.

"We can only begin to imagine, Nam Mee, how you felt," I said.

"I'm sure you didn't sleep much," Cameron added, softly.

"Hardly at all, for days and days!"

Nam Mee continued quietly, "Of course, I hope he will write to me himself. Oh, if only I could hear his voice one more time. Perhaps, even—oh, maybe someday he will want to see me. There are many things I need to say to him. But now, somehow, I can let him go without the pain I've felt. You are his parents. I'm glad and thankful for that. Even if I never see him, if that is never possible, it will be all right. I'm all right!" Tears were our only response. Looking at Cameron and me, Nam Mee then added with her quiet beauty, "It's hard to believe, but right now I have a kind of peace inside me that I didn't think I would ever know again."

I could sense it. I could feel the calming love present in that room. It was a mysterious, sacred moment we shared. It was time . . . out of time!

We were oblivious to the passing of time during those few hours. The sisters had a train to catch back to Nagoya. The two women rose slowly from their cushions. Each of us knew that there was much more to say and share.

I suddenly realized that I had never even served the tea!

In Japanese Cameron thanked Nam Mee's sister for coming with her. Turning, he held out his arms to Nam Mee. "This is a wonderful beginning," he said. "We are your friends, always!" Then he hugged her.

As Cameron stepped aside, Nam Mee's eyes met mine. In that moment, all our shared pain and hurt and joy and hope surfaced. We were two mothers, bound together by one child. As we embraced, Nam Mee's moist cheek touched mine. Our tears ran together, and she whispered, slowly, in my ear, "Please, tell me one thing... did he cry that first night?"

I looked into her eyes.

"Yes," I answered, "Young Ho cried all night long."

Chapter 10

Mark did not yet know that Cameron and I had met his birth mother. I wanted to tell him about it in person and with the utmost care. I had not seen him since he'd left Japan for college nine months earlier.

Now, ten days after that eventful encounter in Kyoto, I was in Massachusetts visiting family. Cameron remained in Japan for the summer, and Mark had been participating in a marine biology course in the Bahamas. He planned to join me in New England and then return with me to Minnesota.

In a borrowed car, I went alone to pick him up at the airport. The hour-long trip back to my sister's house seemed the best opportunity to tell him of our remarkable meeting. He knew only what I had written six weeks earlier:

> "We've had word that the adoption agency in Korea has located members of your family living in Pusan, and they know where your birth mother is living. Hope to have more news for you by the time I return."

On top of my open tote bag lay the envelope that Nam Mee had sent us in Japan. Enclosed were copies of my correspondence with her and the photographs from Korea. I planned to reach for the envelope at just the right time and hand it to Mark as we moved northward on Interstate 95. I tried to imagine how he would take it. How would I feel if I were to receive such news?

I parked the car and headed for the terminal. I noticed that the muscles of my jaw were tight, so I relaxed them, but I realized as I walked that they were tight again. "Calm down. He doesn't know what you're about to tell him. Relax!" I admonished myself.

The plane arrived on time, and Mark, among the first passengers to exit, came smiling towards me. His skin, beautifully bronzed, set off those dark eyes and finely chiseled features.

"Hi," he said cheerfully.

"Hi! It's wonderful to see you, Mark! Hope you had a great time down there? You look great! Dad sends his love." I was talking too fast as we awkwardly tried to exchange hugs amidst knapsack, bulging bundles, and boyish reticence.

"Here, I brought you something," he said. He reached into an oversized shopping bag and pulled out an immense conch shell. The shell's rough, chalk-like, spiny exterior contrasted markedly with the smooth, iridescent mother-of-pearl within its swirls, spiraling inward to a concealed center. I looked at this gift with utter amazement. Nothing I could imagine symbolized more vividly the unfolding, the coming together of Mark's life.

"I just found it on the beach yesterday," he said in the joking voice I had missed for these past months. "It must have washed up the night before. You can put it in the bay window with your other shells."

Loaded down with bags, we made our way toward the far reaches of Parking Lot D. I asked if he wanted to drive, but he admitted he was bushed after a final night's celebration. We tossed his gear into the trunk. After settling into the driver's seat, I placed my satchel carefully over the hump on the floor next to Mark's sprawling legs. I glanced down quickly. The envelope was still right on top.

I needed a bridge before jumping headlong into what was coming. I asked about the program. "The students were great," he told me. "And there were two really cute girls. The prof was okay, but his wife always thought we were about to commit a felony." We talked about Cameron,

Mark's brothers and sisters, and about the New England relatives Mark would be visiting.

Finally, we were within thirty minutes of our destination. Mark adjusted the seat backwards. With a quick glance sideways I could see he was about to close his eyes. I decided the right moment had arrived.

"Mark, I've got exciting news for you!" I said a little too brightly. He stared ahead. Did he already know what was coming?

"We've been in touch with your Korean family," I told him. "Ten days ago your birth mother, Nam Mee, and your aunt came to see us at our house in Kyoto."

Mark looked at me in astonishment.

"She brought pictures of you when you were a baby and a small boy. We showed her snapshots of you and our whole family. She especially wanted to know about you and Alex. She brought gifts for both of you. They stayed for almost two hours and then caught a train back to Nagoya where your aunt lives. Nam Mee returned to Korea by military plane."

Mark's seat jerked to its upright position.

He was looking at me intently.

I told him that Nam Mee was married to a serviceman in the U.S. Air Force. "She is a good person, Mark. We liked her very much. You look quite a bit like her." My hand reached for the long white envelope I'd placed within easy reach. "This is for you," I said, handing it to him. "There are letters and pictures and copies of my letters to her."

Mark picked up the three photographs, lingering over each but especially the one of Nam Mee. He asked about the children in one of the pictures. "They are your cousins who live in Pusan. Remember, where our ferry docked? And that is your grandmother sitting at the table with them. I'm sorry she is no longer alive."

He read the letters, then put his hands on them as he laid them on his lap. We moved along the freeway, sharing the silence.

He was wide-awake. He said quietly, "It's amazing, absolutely amazing! I can't believe it!" He shook his head back and forth, laughing softly, trying to comprehend what he had heard and seen in the last few minutes.

"You have her eyes, Mark. Can you see that?" I asked.

"Yup, not bad," he said. We both laughed.

"She'd like to hear from you. Perhaps someday you'll meet her. Would you like that?" (Martha, don't push, I thought.)

He made a slight shrug of the shoulders. The seat back went down again, and Mark closed his eyes.

Family conversations and high-spirited events occupied our time and attention for the next few days. No one spoke to him of this recent news. I had asked them not to. Mark and I returned to the Midwest.

Over the summer we had no further conversations concerning Nam Mee. Mark would bring her up, I thought, when he was ready. But in his room—on the night table next to his bed—lay the envelope I had given him in the car.

Eighteen months passed. Mark received a birthday card from Nam Mee in July. Holiday greetings were exchanged in mid-December. Three beautiful Korean quilts arrived by sea mail at Christmas.

One Sunday afternoon in the fall of 1986, I was in the midst of mopping up a flooded basement after three days of heavy rain. Wearing rubber boots, I ran up two flights of stairs to get a larger pail, more towels, and a second mop. Four steps back down to the basement the phone rang. I sighed, knowing I couldn't ignore it. A friend who was coming to help me had said she would call. I hastened up the stairs to answer the call in our bedroom. Shifting my paraphernalia to my right hand, I grabbed the phone and answered, expecting my friend to tell me whether her water-extracting machine was working. Hearing only an unclear response, I realized it was not the anticipated call. I started over.

"Hello," I said, emphasizing the last syllable.

"Hello. This is Nam Mee."

"Oh, hello! How are you? Where are you?" By this time I had dropped to a sitting position on the bed, my implements at my feet.

"I'm calling from Hawaii. I just want you to know that we've been transferred here from Korea. We're at the Air Force base in Honolulu."

"How wonderful!" Hawaii is so much closer than Korea! "When did you move?" She and her husband had been transferred there three months earlier.

"How is your family?" Nam Mee asked.

"Mark has returned to college, his brother also," I told her. "My husband is back in Japan continuing his research, and I am teaching in special education this fall." I asked for her address and telephone number, but I had trouble understanding some of her words. Her husband came on the phone to make sure I had them down correctly. Then I asked if I might speak to Nam Mee again.

A sudden rush of warmth flowed to my cheeks. The whole scene of our Kyoto meeting flooded in on me. I took a deep breath. "Nam Mee, I want you to know again that our meeting with you in Japan was a momentous event in our lives. We will never forget it."

"Me, too," she answered warmly.

After a moment, I continued. "I'll be joining my husband in Japan early in January. On the way I plan to stop over in Hawaii. I'd like to see you again."

"Please come! I'd like that," she said.

"Thank you. I'll let you know where I'll be staying and the dates. Thanks again for calling. I hope to see you in a few months."

"Bye. See you in January."

"Goodbye, Nam Mee."

I hurried back to the basement. I sang every song I could remember from *South Pacific* as I continued cleaning up. Hawaii seemed practically next door!

When Mark came home the next weekend, I said I had a surprise for him. I told him about the phone call. "Maybe you could visit her there sometime," I offered.

He gave me a quick hug. "Yup, maybe. Hawaii! That's cool," he replied, as he collected his tennis racquet.

열하나 *Chapter 11*

In a letter to Nam Mee in early December, I spelled out my plans for being in Honolulu. I invited her, and her husband, if possible, to join me for brunch at the hotel where I'd be staying. I wrote that I would telephone her a few days before my departure.

Four days before I was to leave, dozens of items still remained on my to-do list. Doggedly, I pushed to get things done. Halfway down my list in bold letters I read: "Call Nam Mee." I glanced at the clock on the stove. "Now's a good time." I picked up my address book from the pile of essentials on the kitchen table and found her number. Suddenly a thought came full force... with implications. In a few moments I hoped I would be talking with Mark's mother.

Suddenly, I opened the door to the den. There Mark, home for the holidays, sat mesmerized by a pre-Superbowl football game.

"Mark," I said nonchalantly, "I'm about to call Nam Mee in Hawaii. How about saying 'Hello?'"

He winced. His startled eyes quickly focused on my face. "But what would I say?" he snapped.

"Oh, you could wish her a Happy New Year," I offered. "How about that?"

Mark shrugged his shoulders, but he didn't say no. His gaze returned to the television screen, and he said nothing more.

I went back to the kitchen and picked up the phone. Seconds after my fingers touched the last of eleven numbers I heard Nam Mee's voice. I reiterated my plans and my hope that she would come to my hotel.

"Please stay with *me*," she replied. "There's plenty of room. My husband is in Arizona for three-week maneuvers."

I demurred. "Thank you, but the first night I'll stay in the hotel I think. I'll have to get a good rest. Then we can see." She told me she would take a bus to my hotel. I said, "Oh, great! You can come for brunch. It will be so good to see you again, Nam Mee."

Then I walked with the long-corded phone toward the den. Opening the door, my pulse quickening, I gambled. "Mark is right here. He wants to say something to you."

With my hand over the receiver I leaned into the den. "Mark, it's Nam Mee," I said, nodding toward another phone within his reach. Mark had the look of a frightened animal who is suddenly trapped. I said a silent prayer.

Mark fumbled for the phone. Then he uttered, awkwardly, "Hello, this is Mark."

I hastily retreated to the kitchen, my hand still tight around the receiver. Suddenly it was I who felt trapped, caught between being a caretaker and an intruder. I froze, but hung on.

"Hello, Mark," said Nam Mee, her voice low and gentle.

"Hello," he answered. "Merry Christmas, I mean Happy New Year."

All three of us laughed.

Nam Mee spoke slowly, "I hope you had … had a good Christmas."

"Yes, it was fine. How about you?" he answered.

"Fine." She paused. "Mark, why don't you come to Hawaii with your Mom?"

Lightheartedly he replied, "I can't because of college. I'll come later. Maybe in May or June."

There was silence for many seconds. Then in quiet, distinct words, Nam Mee said, "I want to see you."

"Me, too," came the whispered answer from our son.

Neither one said anything else.

Finally I said quietly, "I think it will be wonderful when you two can see each other again."

" It will be… it will be so," Nam Mee was crying. "I never thought I'd hear his voice, ever again. Mark. Goodbye, Mark."

"Goodbye. Happy New Year." The receiver in the den clicked off.

"Yes, Happy New Year, Nam Mee," I interjected, once again attempting a sprightly tone. "I'll see you in a few days—on Sunday, in fact. Nam Mee, goodbye."

I replaced the phone and stood briefly at the open door of the den. Mark did not look up, perhaps he didn't know I was there. He stared intently at the television.

I took our golden retriever Liza for a long walk. When we returned, Mark was putting on his jacket. "I have to get back to Minneapolis," he told me. "I need to be at work in an hour. I'll stay up there in my apartment tonight. I'll be back in the morning—I'm playing hockey here with some guys at eleven o'clock."

I was fixing myself a cup of coffee when Mark walked in the back door the following morning.

"How about having some of this mocha java?" I asked, glad to show him I appreciated the special coffee he'd given me for Christmas.

"Great!" He called Liza, picked up a Frisbee and disappeared into the backyard. "I'll let you know when it's ready!" I called after him.

When the brew was done, I filled two mugs and placed them opposite each other at the kitchen table. We chatted about his job. Next I read him the letter that had just come from Cameron, who'd returned to Japan after Christmas. I then took my mug in both hands and leaned forward, resting my elbows on the table.

"Mark, I hope you don't mind my asking—but I've wondered over and over since yesterday. Can I ask? What was it like, how did you feel, when you heard Nam Mee's voice?"

Mark regarded me closely from across the table. He replied, sternly, "Well, you sure didn't give me much choice in the matter. Do you know that?"

"I know," I said, "Please forgive me. We had talked about your speaking to her before I made the call. I knew you were hesitant, and I really thought you needed a gentle push. It was risky, Mark. I knew that. But I had to trust that it would be okay."

Mark tipped his mug straight up, then went to get more coffee from the pot. When he sat down again, he began speaking dreamily, almost as if in a trance. Often half phrases tumbled out in quiet tones. His lowered eyes fixed on his mug.

"Yeah, on the way back—when I was driving up to my job—and I had this great music on, I mean, I just couldn't believe it. I couldn't believe I actually heard her voice! I remember now when I first came here sometimes dreaming about her calling to me. Yesterday was the first time since I was five years old, now I'm twenty-two. It was incredible. I was on the biggest high. I thought the car was going to fly. I couldn't believe how I felt. It was something in her voice. And when she said, 'Why don't you come to Hawaii?' and 'I want to see you.' I can't explain. I can't put it in words. You, nobody, could know what it was like."

We sat there without speaking. Finally, I said, "Thanks, Mark, thanks for telling me."

" I needed to tell someone." He then added, "That was an important thing to do—to talk to her, I mean."

"I think you're right," I answered with profound relief. I was on my own incredible high. "It was a good step to take. Things will be easier, now that the door is opened. I'm excited for you, Mark. Dad will be, too."

I got up to stir the soup simmering on the stove and asked more briskly, "What do you think about May or June? Is that when you'd like to meet her?"

"Yup," Mark said quickly. "Maybe right after exams. Yeah, I'd like that. It won't be like going to Hawaii for a vacation, that's for sure."

"I know," I answered. "But that's why it's good you've at least talked to her." I waited a few minutes before continuing, aware I might be pushing too fast. But this would not be easy by letter or phone, and in forty-eight hours I was leaving for Japan. "Maybe you don't know now and, anyway, you don't have to say yet. You'll want to think about it, I'm sure. But I need to at least raise the question. Can you... can you imagine ahead to the spring?" I almost stuttered. "Would you want me to be in Hawaii when you go to see Nam Mee? Or do you want to be there by yourself?"

Without delay, Mark responded, "I want you there in Hawaii, but I want to see her first by myself."

What a relief. Honest words, straight from the heart.

We talked about when college would be out, and I marked the date in my book. Mark turned sideways in his chair and threw his leg across the seat of an adjacent chair. For once he didn't seem eager to get on with his own agenda.

"Did her voice sound familiar at all?" I asked.

"Oh, *Mom!*" he exclaimed, "no, not at all. It's been a long, long time." Then looking at me he added, "Mom, I wonder if I'd even recognize her *face*. Maybe she's forgotten mine, even my little boy one."

We sat quietly before speaking again.

I shifted around in my chair, tucking one leg underneath, and said, "You know, once I remember you told your brother that you didn't have a mother. You told him you had an older sister and that you used to visit her on weekends. It was when you were living most of the time with your grandmother. Dad and I thought that perhaps this 'sister' might actually be your mother. Maybe your family was trying to ease some of the pain of the coming separation.

"Do you remember going often with your 'older sister?'" I thought if he could remember it might help him to understand.

Mark turned sideways in his chair and gazed out the bay window. His hand reached out over the dozens of sea treasures in the space by the windows. He picked up the largest one, the conch shell he had brought me from the Bahamas. He held it in his hands while his finger moved over the smooth coral-tinted swirl hidden inside.

"I remember once, this woman—I guess she was my sister, or I thought she was—she came … and there was a man. They took me to a pool. There was running water, like a waterfall, and I waded in it. It was outside the village, maybe in a park."

He put the conch shell down on the table where we sat. He reached for a scratch piece of paper and drew a sketch. Retracing his steps with a pencil, he said, "We walked along this diagonal path out from where I lived with my grandmother and came to a pretty big pool. I took off my sandals and went in the pool. I tried to catch one of the little fish. I'd have one in my hand, but it would wiggle away and splash back into the pool. Then they brought me back to *Hal moni.*"

Startled, he looked at me with big eyes. In almost a whisper, he said, "I didn't even know I remembered the word for grandmother, *hal moni!*"

열둘 *Chapter 12*

When I awoke on Sunday morning in Honolulu, I felt peaceful and rested. There was time for a swim before Nam Mee arrived. At nine o'clock I went down to the lobby, armed with postcards and pen, to await her. I sat writing where I could look out the open doors to the wide boulevard. Half an hour later I dropped the postcards into a mailbox.

From there I saw three people pause in the parking lot, then move hesitantly toward the hotel entrance. There was a small girl, about three years old, a tall young woman and an older one, all Asian. The older woman and I exchanged glances, looked away and then, simultaneously, turned back again in recognition. I hurried toward Nam Mee, and we embraced awkwardly. Nam Mee looked thinner and younger than I remembered. She was dressed casually, in jeans with a loose-fitting white sweatshirt top and leather thongs. Her deep eyes glistened, especially when she smiled. The full warm tone of her supple skin was enhanced by thick black hair, now shorter and falling naturally in soft waves. Her manner was one of unaffected ease, with a touch of deference.

Nam Mee introduced the young woman, Marie, a neighbor who had offered to help her find the hotel. I put my hand on top of the young child's ebony locks and said, "Hello! What's your name?" Her eyes fell demurely to the pavement. I looked to Marie for a clue, but much to my astonishment it was Nam Mee who said, as she took the small hand in hers and we moved toward the hotel entrance, "This is my, our, daughter—Wendy. We adopted her last year before leaving Korea."

Nam Mee's eyes looked directly into mine as I stopped walking. "How absolutely wonderful!" I exclaimed.

Clutching her Cabbage Patch doll, Wendy eyed me cautiously, offering the suggestion of a smile. I dropped down and she came forward to receive my hug.

The four of us sat at a small round table on the arbored terrace. We ordered from the ample brunch menu. Wendy sat tucked in beside Nam Mee on a large wrought-iron chair.

"Wendy and I will share," announced Nam Mee. "She's already had some breakfast."

We talked easily, of Mark and his activities and studies, of his brothers and sisters, our husbands. Nam Mee often punctuated her words with an extra syllable at the end.

Wendy and Marie left us to walk along the beach. I looked across the table at my beautiful friend. "I'm so happy to see you again. You are looking very well, Nam Mee."

For the second time that morning, I heard the unexpected.

"I am feeling better now," she answered. "But I learned last April that I have breast cancer.

"It's okay now," she continued, "the doctors are sure they got it all. I lost a lot of weight when I was in the hospital for two months in Korea. Then I had radiation treatments here at the military hospital. It's one of the best there is, you know. My husband will stay in the service a few years more, even though he's had twenty years. That way we can have expert medical care."

I expressed my deep concern, but once she had told me of her illness, I could tell she was eager to change the subject.

"Now, how about coming back to the base with us and spending the night?" she asked. "We're very close to the airport, and a Korean friend of mine said she would be happy to bring you there to catch your plane to Osaka in the morning."

I couldn't say no.

I checked out of the hotel, and soon the four of us were on the hour-long bus ride through the tourist-laden thoroughfares of Honolulu, headed for the military base on its outskirts. I took from my satchel a children's book (intended for a young friend in Japan) and gave it to Wendy, who now sat on Nam Mee's lap while she turned the pages.

We passed through the security check at the base, got off the bus in the residential area and walked the short distance to one of many courtyards with attached units on three sides. I took off my shoes inside the door. Nam Mee then gave me a tour of their attractive home. We stopped outside the last of four rooms on the second floor.

"This is my Korean room. I come up here a lot. I can get special Korean programs on that small TV over there," Nam Mee said, pointing to a set on the floor. Against the walls were two black lacquered chests with designs of inlaid mother-of-pearl. Shelves were decorated with Korean art objects. A low dressing table, also lacquered, held a tall narrow mirror. On the floor in front of it lay a vivid blue satin pillow, elaborately embroidered.

"I fix my hair here. And I will sleep here tonight," Nam Mee told me, pointing to the futon bedding in the corner. "I want you to sleep in my bed." She pointed to the largest room.

I protested saying that I'd enjoy sleeping on the futon, but I soon deferred to her wishes.

We went downstairs and sat at the large dining table, whose lace tablecloth was protected by clear plastic. Nam Mee stepped around to the adjacent kitchen and poured us each a Diet Coke.

"Nam Mee," I said in a concerned voice, "you have lost quite a bit of weight since we saw you in Japan. I hope you're not losing any more."

"No," she said, "I've gained some back." Then, as if she needed to tell me, she added, "They took some out up here. You want to see?" Before I could answer, she lifted her loose-fitting top and adjusted her bra to show me the incision that had been made across the top of her breast. The whole area was darkened, almost bluish in color.

"That's from the radiation. I have to be careful to stay out of the sun. They took some from under my arm and I go back for checkups every few months." She put her top down, looked at me, and said, "That was a funny thing to do, I mean showing you that, but you're family and I wanted to."

I got up and kissed her on the cheek.

"Thanks, Nam Mee," I said, "thanks for saying that."

"Well," she grinned, "we're more than friends!"

"Yes," I agreed, "we are more than friends!"

Wendy came into the house with her playmate. They sat down with us for a cold drink and a cookie. Between mouthfuls, Wendy, said to her friend Jason as she looked at me, "She's my grandma, you know, but I don't know which one."

Nam Mee and I laughed. Nam Mee shrugged her shoulders. "I didn't tell her that. She figured it out."

"Perfect," I said, "Instant grandmother!" Wendy and Jason slid off their chairs and disappeared outside.

For the next hour Nam Mee, often searching for the right word, told me how Wendy came to be their daughter.

In July 1984, about two months after we met her in Kyoto, she and her husband were living on an American base outside Pusan, Korea. In the dark early hours Nam Mee was awakened by the long, insistent ringing of the front doorbell. She sat up in bed, poked her sleeping husband, and swung her legs to the floor. Hastily but half asleep, she threw on her summer robe, descended the stairs to the outside door and asked in Korean, "Who's there?" When there was no answer she repeated the question loudly in English. By this time her husband was at her side urging caution. Peering out a small rectangular window near the top of the door, he said he could see no one.

Then he opened the door carefully, alert and wary, as befitted a master sergeant.

There, under the stars, they saw before them—in a woven basket placed on the ground in front of their cement step—a small form wrapped in a large blanket. They heard quiet whimpering. Nam Mee dropped to her knees beside the baby. She saw dark, wet eyes peering at her uncertainly, framed by thick black hair.

She quickly brought the basket inside and lifted the tiny girl. Nam Mee and her husband were speechless. The baby was about eighteen months old, clad in a summer sleeping garment. A half-filled bottle of milk was tucked inside the light blanket. When Nam Mee picked the child up she saw a folded piece of paper lying under the covering. On it was written, in black crayon: "Ples took care me."

Nam Mee's husband called base security while Nam Mee discarded the contents of the bottle, warmed fresh milk, and offered it to the child as she held her. Miraculously, the child drank quietly and soon fell asleep. Holding the sleeping child, Nam Mee lay down with her on a futon her husband had brought from upstairs. Soon security personnel came. They would return later, they said, seeing that the child was in good hands.

Nam Mee stayed beside the baby, her body curled around the small form. Nam Mee slept fitfully. Astonishment at the night's events aroused her from her dreamlike state several times. As she lay next to this unknown child, she remembered a time long ago when she had slept next to Mark.

The next morning's investigation revealed that the child was the daughter of a young clerical worker. This teen-age, single mother had found it impossible to care for her child and become distraught. Through a co-worker who lived on the base she sought a family who could care for the baby. The co-worker, whom Nam Mee and her husband barely knew, suggested them. Theirs was a good marriage but without children, the mother was told.

Nam Mee continued. "I didn't tell you this before, but ten years ago I had to have the operation where you can't ever have children again."

"A hysterectomy?" I asked.

"Yes, that was it." Then she added, "So even if I had changed my mind I couldn't have had a child." She was referring to what she had told her husband before they married: that she would never bear another child because she had sent her only child away. "I still feel so guilty about what I had to do for Mark. It never leaves me. My husband and I decided to raise this little girl. It was our only chance to be parents. We named her after my husband's sister in America. She's a good girl, and I can't believe how we love her."

Although an agreement about the baby was reached, nine months later the birth mother took her back. That event threw Nam Mee into a sea of emotions in which she nearly drowned. Terrible thoughts haunted her. Was this punishment for what she had done years before to Mark? She agonized over her cruel fate. She felt she deserved to continue to suffer for her terrible deed. At the same time she sympathized with Wendy's birth mother. She knew how the child's mother felt. The same intense, agonized longing had besieged her after Mark's departure.

Within a few weeks the child begged to return to Nam Mee and her husband. Having grown accustomed to their love and attention— and perhaps for additional reasons—she was not happy in her original circumstances. The anquished young mother, accepting her inability to give the child what she needed, surrendered the little girl a second time. A month before leaving Korea for Hawaii, the new family of three appeared before the magistrate in Pusan, and the adoption was legally sealed.

Nam Mee looked out at the children playing in the backyard. "I sometimes think about Wendy's birth mother and how she's doing."

She paused, then looked at me. "You and your husband have raised my child," she said. "We will raise this one." My heart answered: How wonderful for Wendy *and* for you!

Without speaking of it we both seemed conscious of the limited time we had left together.

"Do you really think Mark will come here in May?" Nam Mee asked.

"Yes, I do. He was the one who said it. He was so glad you asked him. It meant a lot to him to talk with you. I think he's ready. How about you?" I ventured.

"Oh," she burst forth. "I don't know… I mean, yes. But do you think he has forgiven me for sending him away? What does he think? I just never thought I'd see him again, ever."

"He wants to come, Nam Mee," I told her. "It's important for him also, to see you. He doesn't think it will be easy, but I know he wants to come. He told me so before I left."

Her palms went to her temples and she pressed her hands around the top of her head. "I can't believe it, I just can't, after all these years."

I decided to tell her what I had been thinking, wanting her to be prepared when the time came. "Mark may need to ask you questions about his father."

From the look on her face, I knew my words caused her great pain. She put her hands in front of her mouth and protested. "I can't say anything. I can't talk about that."

I tried to calm her. "You don't have to tell me a thing. I just want you to know that Mark might need to ask. He's never said anything to me about it." I reached for her hand. "I didn't mean to upset you."

That evening after I had read Wendy a story and her mother had tucked her in bed, we opened the large photo album that had been brought out earlier in the day.

As the oversized pages were turned, revealing faded or yellowing images, Nam Mee told me more about her family. She was born in 1933 into a large family. Her father was a good and respected man, she said. He ran a shop where different kinds of fabric were sold. "My father prospered in his business before the war, but then everything changed. We had practically nothing. There was little to eat. But my mother, she always took care of people. If my mother had half a cup of something, she would offer half of it to someone who needed it. Always, every day, there was a knock on the door. People came begging and she gave them something. These weren't poor poor people, but they had left their homes in North Korea. Often they had escaped with little more than the clothes on their backs. My mother, I think she was the kindest person I ever knew."

I smiled. "I'll bet you're like her."

"No, not really. I'm more like my father."

"Hmmm, how so?"

"I speak out what I think. I used to be told I shouldn't do that. But I can't help it. It is unusual for a woman to do that in Korea. Sometimes my family and others didn't know what to do with me. When Mark was first born he didn't look so different from other children, but before long it was obvious he was different.

"A few weeks after I brought him to my father's home in Pusan, my father asked my mother, 'What is it about this child?' My mother did not tell him that his father was an American. He would not understand. After my father's question, I knew I had to leave. I moved to Ulsan to spare my father from the truth. Before I went, some of my siblings railed at me saying, 'You are no longer a member of this family.' They told me to take my name off the family register. Two brothers forced me to go to the municipal office and saw that my name was removed."

By this act, Nam Mee wiped out her legal identity, an extreme deed in a country where family registers are sacrosanct. In the months and years that followed, isolated for the most part from her kin and shunned by others, Nam Mee often thought of taking her life and that of her child. She told me of her confused mind and her weary, grieving heart.

Eventually, she moved to Seoul, and encouraged by an older woman, she obtained work in the commissary at a U.S. Army base. Her mother, now widowed, had come to help her. Sometimes her son visited her at her job. The young army recruits played ball with him and gave him sweets. For a while things looked brighter for them. But as her handsome child neared school age, her despair returned and heightened.

"People at the base told me what a beautiful child he was. And he was so smart you only had to tell him something once. He always remembered. But outside the base, where we lived in a tiny place by a stream, people would point at him and look at me with scorn. Little boys made fun of him and called him names. 'GI kid,' they said, and pushed him around. I got him a small bicycle somehow, and the boys smashed it. When his grandmother was there, he often crawled onto her lap and she would rub his back for a long time."

Friends on the base began talking to Nam Mee about overseas adoption. For a long time the very idea seemed abhorrent. She couldn't imagine life without Mark. One day, a woman from an adoption agency, alerted by someone on the base, came to talk with Nam Mee about the possibility. The agency representative pointed out that Mark was close to school age. She forecast a dim future in Korea.

The woman came twice in two weeks. Nam Mee finally came to see adoption as the lesser of two evils, but she fought it the whole way. When the agency told her they would need to house the child six months before his departure, she refused. She told them that she herself would take him to the hospital and other places where tests and papers needed to be taken care of.

"Will you sign the papers?" the social worker asked. Nam Mee promised she would.

Thus, except for a mandatory ten-day observation period at the adoption facility, mother and child remained together. After Nam Mee's father's death, her mother had come to live with them and helped to care for the child. During the last few weeks before his departure, Nam Mee brought Mark to the adoption center each day for an orientation with other children leaving for America. They were taught how to use a spoon and fork, instructed in a few English words, and shown pictures of the United States. Each night, Nam Mee fetched her son, and they returned to their small quarters.

Nam Mee turned a few pages of the photo album, then stopped. She explained that the dozen small black-and-white pictures on the two pages in front of us were all taken the morning of the day Mark left.

"I took a whole roll," she said softly.

Indeed, there Mark stood in the dark shorts, blue turtleneck, white stockings, and brown moccasins in which we had met him. As if to preserve, to cherish, each part of him, Nam Mee had taken pictures of him from every angle. They would be all she had.

Looking up at me, Nam Mee said quietly, "Do you remember how he looked when he arrived?" She then added quickly, "And did you like him right away?"

"I'll never forget our first glimpse of him," I answered. "Yes, he was wearing exactly those clothes." I pointed to one of the photos in front of us. I still have those little moccasins he wore. They're on the top shelf of my linen closet."

"Did he smile when he saw you? And did you like him right away?" she asked again.

"No, he didn't smile for a while. But we, we thought he was wonderful from the beginning! We also knew he was a very tired and confused little boy. He finally took Cameron's hand, but his small body was as rigid as a board. He fell asleep on the hour-long ride back to our home."

Nam Mee told me about her last moments with Young Ho—Mark—at the Seoul terminal. When they got to the airport, others from the adoption center were already there. Of the thirteen children in all, nine were babies. Nam Mee and her son stayed apart from the rest. Mark, wide-eyed and curious, was fascinated by all that was going on at that place of departure. Nam Mee sat back on her heels beside him. She asked, "Do, do you want to go? Or do you just want to ride on the plane?"

"I want to take a look," he answered, with his confusion showing on his small face. "I don't know," he added. He didn't understand what she was trying to say.

One of the social workers came toward them. "It's time," she said.

Nam Mee looked up from her crouched position beside her child. "He's not sure he wants to go." She put her arms more tightly around him.

"I'm sorry, Nam Mee," the woman said in a kind voice. "It's too late. His family in America is waiting for him. It's time for him to board."

The woman leaned down, connected her hand with his, and gently led him toward the plane.

Nam Mee leaned back in her chair and looked at me. "Then it was over. He just said, 'Goodbye.'"

"'Goodbye, be a good boy.' Those were my very last words to him."

Halfway to the bulkhead leading inside the huge jetliner, Mark turned. He cupped his hand to the side of his mouth, as if he were already at a distance, and called to the still-crouched figure he had left behind. "When I grow up I'm going to be a pilot, and I'll come back to get you."

Then slowly Nam Mee added, "He stepped onto the airplane and was gone from sight."

열셋 *Chapter 13*

In May 1987, seventeen years later to the month, this boy, now grown to manhood, walked off another airplane into the airport at Honolulu. On that day Mark—Young Ho—and his first mother, Nam Mee, were reunited. Her husband and their daughter Wendy met him, too.

Later Mark was able to tell me about it.

He had just finished his final exams the day he flew to Honolulu. He was exhausted. Not only had he been cramming for tests, but for weeks he'd been enveloped by the tumultuous event about to unfold in his life. As the plane began its descent into Honolulu, he closed his eyes and saw himself reaching for the life jacket beneath his seat. He was not at all sure he would survive the first moments of this reunion. It was the most difficult threshold he had to cross. He desperately wanted that scene behind him!

My plane from Osaka arrived eighteen hours later. Mark, Nam Mee, and Wendy met me. I bit my lip hard as I walked toward that trio. Mark, towering over Wendy, came toward me holding her hand. I had not seen Mark for almost six months. He picked Wendy up and they gave me a collective hug. I turned to Nam Mee and put my arms around her and held her. No words seemed adequate.

I was not surprised by the tenseness I saw in Mark's face, particularly around the eyes. In their too-focused gaze I saw a hint of the strain he was under. Beneath their smiles, he and Nam Mee both looked extremely tired. When Mark was fetching my luggage, I was finally able to say to Nam Mee, "In all of human experience, I cannot envision a more emotional situation than the one you and Mark are now going through."

She nodded, but could not speak.

We checked my heavy bags at the airport, and Mark drove us to Nam Mee's home on the base. Later I would go to my hotel, while Mark stayed with Nam Mee, her husband, and Wendy on the base.

On the way to the base, with Mark driving, mixed feelings raced through my own mind. I saw mother and son together and thought, "What a wonderful scene!" I also saw and felt their discomfort. In the back seat Wendy and I chatted about her school and friends. Then she looked up at me and said, "I love my brother!" Quickly she added, "Did you know he cried at the airport yesterday?"

Mark shot a quick glance in our direction. Unembarrassed, he pursed his lips together and nodded.

"That's good. I'm glad," I said.

Nam Mee, sitting beside Mark up front, looked straight ahead and said softly, "I cried, too."

In the kitchen of her house Nam Mee busied herself fixing a cold drink for me and *kimchi* for Mark. She put a large bowl in front of him. Mark ate the pickled cabbage, strong with garlic, as if it was his favorite food. "This is his second helping today. He remembers how much he liked it when he was a little boy... Right, Mark?" she said to him.

"Yup, I love the stuff!"

"I'll have to make some more in a hurry." And she put what little remained into the small separate refrigerator where her husband insisted she keep the pungent concoction.

I was beginning to relax. "He'll keep you busy while he's here," I laughed. "He is a bottomless pit and *always* has room for more." Mark, too, began to look more relaxed as he went out to push Wendy on the swing.

On our way to the base club for dinner that evening, Nam Mee sat in the back with Mark while her husband Ed drove. I was half-turned in the bucket seat up front chatting with them. Nam Mee reached over and gently took Mark's hand in hers. "Your hand, it is so big," she said. "It is huge!" She took her finger and—starting with his little one— moved hers with great tenderness up and down each one of his long, slender fingers and over his thumb. "Your fingers, your hand, they are beautiful."

The next day Mark, Wendy, and Nam Mee came to my hotel. Mark played with Wendy in the shallow water of the hotel beach, supporting her as she dog-paddled beside him. Nam Mee and I sat out of the sun on a wall at the edge of the sand.

It was the first time she and I had been alone since the reunion. By this time, all vestiges of my earlier doubts had been dispelled. We sat side-by-side watching the scene in front of us. Neither of us spoke. The silence, in a mysterious way, expressed the bond that existed between us.

After several moments Nam Mee said in a hushed voice, "He is such a fine, good person. And he has a wonderfully handsome face! All through the years I tried to imagine what he looked like, and what kind of a person he had become, at eight, ten, twelve, fifteen."

I could feel her deep yearning. I said, softly. "And I, I was across the world trying to imagine your face, Nam Mee. I wanted to know who you were. I knew you could never forget your child."

She continued, "I thought about him every single day of my life. All I had were the early pictures, the last ones taken the day he left.

"And, oh, I worried so when he was in his teens, especially about drugs and all the bad things that I know happen to so many. I tried to keep my hope alive but, oh it was so hard." She turned to me with moist eyes. "But he's all right, isn't he?"

"Yes, yes, Nam Mee, he is very much all right. And, perhaps, in some mysterious way, your keeping him close in your thoughts helped him to be strong." I smiled and put my hand on hers.

"He's your son," she continued. "You raised him. I just needed to see him once." Her tears came. "I needed to know he's all right. It is hard for me to believe he's here."

I turned to face her as we sat on the wall. The depth of my feeling for her at that moment overwhelmed me. I took her two hands in mine.

"Nam Mee," I said, "he is not *our* child. He does not belong to us. He is God's child. He is a precious and good human being. And both of us have been his mother."

"I feel so guilty about what I did. I know he probably wants to talk about it before he goes back in a few days, but I'm too full. I hope he will forgive me, but I can't talk about the past with him now." Her husband had that morning told me that he was concerned about Nam Mee's emotional overload. He said she would need time to make sense of all the feelings she was trying to cope with.

We continued to watch Mark and Wendy, now building a super-structure in the sand that was being lapped by the slowly rising tide. I hoped he was as absorbed in it as Wendy appeared to be. He needed to be warmed by the sun and by the moment.

"You must be feeling sadness as well as joy in seeing him," I ventured. "Surely, it must be painful for you to think of all the years you've missed sharing his life, seeing him grow year by year, not being with him after all the closeness you had known. It must be very hard."

She spoke in almost a whisper. "Yes, that's how I feel. Part of it is," she hesitated, "part of it is something I haven't told you yet. Six months after I sent him away, Ed asked me to marry him. I had known him earlier as a friend, and then he was sent to Okinawa for two years. He knew Mark when he was a little boy around three. He used to play with him sometimes when I brought him on the base with me, when I worked in the mess hall. But at the time, Ed was just an acquaintance. When he came back to the base in Korea after those two years away, one of the first things he asked me was, 'Where is your son?'"

Her pain cut deep inside me. I knew what was coming. "Do you see?" she implored. "Soon our relationship became serious, and we made plans to marry. And I told Ed I would never have another child because of sending Mark away. Now I was haunted night and day by the fact that, in my marriage, my son would have been welcomed and loved by my husband. He would have had schooling on the base. There were many children like him whose parents were of different races. His life would have been good, he would have been accepted, and he would have been with me."

Her voice was very sad as she spoke with increasing rapidity, as if all her insides were falling out. She couldn't stop. "Once more I almost went over the edge. I wanted him back. I pestered the agency to tell me where he was in America. I was going to put an ad in the papers if only I could remember the state. I knew it began with M. Was it Michigan, Massachusetts, Minnesota, Montana? I was going to find him, and I was going to ask you to send him back. I could think of nothing else. My husband became alarmed and feared for me and for our marriage. 'You must stop this. You must let him go,' he told me. 'You must put him out of your mind, or you will go out of yours.' He was very firm with me. And so in the end, to save myself, I had to let him go."

A shudder passed through my body. I thought of her agony and in the same breath thought of the agony we would have gone through had she located us and asked for her son back.

During the next afternoon with her, Nam Mee asked me to go with her upstairs to see something in her "Korean Room." It was a small statue of Kannon, the Buddhist figure of mercy and compassion. It had belonged to her grandmother.

"I became a Christian soon after I sent Mark away," she informed me. "I go to a Korean church here, and it is important to me. But this statue will always be important, too. It has comforted me in the many struggles I've been through." She was holding the statue in her hand as she added, "And now, now that I know how much you were thinking all those many years about me and about my pain—somehow that must have helped me survive, too."

We stood facing each other. "Nam Mee," I hesitated. "Nam Mee, I hope you have felt healing these past few days. I hope you no longer feel guilty for having sent Mark away. It was an act of pure and courageous love. You did it for him, in spite of the agony you knew would be yours. You did it because you loved him."

She looked into my eyes. "I didn't know how bad it would be. It nearly killed me." She took a deep breath and her shoulders relaxed a little. "You, your family, have given him so much. I am so grateful. I don't have words."

"And, he has given *us* so much! Nam Mee, you must have some sense of how grateful we are to you. You, not we, gave him the most precious gift—a basic sense of trust in other people and in the world. You gave that to him, we didn't. It was part of Mark when he came to us. It was a miracle, with all the pain in your life and in his, that this life-giving hope and trust were in him. Think of that, Nam Mee! And he has remained trusting and optimistic. Of course, Mark will face struggles in the future as he has in the past. But he has the inner strength to sustain him."

I held her close in my heart as I added, "I hope you can let the guilt go. I don't want you to feel guilty any more."

She put the statue down and stood in front of me. Raising her hands to the top of her head, she moved them slowly down over her shoulders, then close to her body, ending in an outward extended motion. With a comely smile she spoke in a hushed voice.

"It is going… it is going away."

At that moment a shroud that had encased her whole being for a long time seemed to fall away.

The next morning I flew back to the Midwest, one day ahead of schedule. I knew that Nam Mee and Mark deserved and needed time by themselves, without me, so I changed my plans. Mark would have two more days in Hawaii with Nam Mee.

When my plane was aloft, and I had settled back into partial oblivion, I realized how emotionally exhausted I was. My feelings helped me know, at least in part, the impact Nam Mee and Mark's emotions must be having on them—not just over the past few days, but for months, even years, to come—as they would for me.

I had witnessed an extraordinary human drama. For Nam Mee and Mark, the range of feelings were immense, and their interweavings, complex. It would take time to sort them out.

My second night home, I was awakened by the phone. It was Nam Mee. She had just returned from saying goodbye to Mark at the airport. We conversed about things they'd done in their last forty-eight hours together. I thanked her for all she and her husband had done for me and for their warm welcome of Mark. I spoke of how much it must have meant to him.

"Mark told me he'd had a wonderful time, that it had been good but too short," Nam Mee replied. And then she added, "We both knew there was much we could not, did not talk about."

"Another time, perhaps, that will be possible," I offered. "Maybe next time that will be easier to do."

Then her tone changed from one of joyfulness to a quiet, almost reverent tone. "I needed to call you to say the only words I know."

I was not prepared for what came next. In measured words, slowly, softly, in descending cadence, ending in a whisper, she said, "Thank you… thank you… thank you… thank you… thank you… thank you… thank you."

I placed the phone slowly back in its cradle. Then I put on my robe and went out into the warm May night and sat on the stone steps for a very long time, under the stars.

결어 *Afterword: Reflections by Mark*

When I was six years old, living in Korea, my birth mother gave me up for adoption, primarily because I was of mixed heritage, Korean/American. Since Koreans highly prize the purity of their race, I had no chance of going to school or of having other opportunities that children of full Korean background do. Not allowed to be a Korean citizen, my life would have been dismal had I stayed in Korea. Therefore, I was adopted by my current family, who live in Minnesota. My adoptive father teaches at a liberal arts college and my adoptive mother has been a special education teacher at a public elementary school. At the time of adoption, I went from being an only child to being the youngest of five siblings. Now I have two older brothers and two older sisters.

I recognized at an early age the importance of looking toward future challenges, not dwelling on the past. While growing up, I always knew I was adopted, and my parents often spoke of it. Many adopted children find it easy to psych themselves into believing that blood is thicker than water; that their adopted parents do not love them as intensely as they do their biological children. Problems of poor self-esteem, alienation from family, and delinquency in adolescence can all stem from these feelings. Feelings of emptiness and despair are common.

I believe a crucial task for the adopted person (it was certainly true in my case) is to develop his or her own sense of belonging by carving out an appropriate niche for themselves within the family unit.

During adolescence, like others of that age, I focused on issues of who and what I am. Because my parents recognized the pending issues of my self-discovery, a course of events that would change my life forever was put into motion. At the age of nineteen, with my parents, I was fortunate enough to visit Korea and the orphanage at which I once stayed. I took tours of the countryside and went to museums, temples and art exhibits in the capital of Seoul. All of this exposed me to Korean culture and its heritage. Inevitably, this contributed to my developing sense of identity.

Roughly two years after my visit to Korea my birth mother, Nam Mee, was located, and a visit with her was arranged. Many questions were answered, and a relationship was restarted. Having since reestablished connection with Nam Mee, I have found some amazing twists in her life. Ironically, Nam Mee ended up getting married to an American Air Force sergeant, nine months after giving me up for adoption. I had missed being part of an entirely different life by nine months! And, also ironically, while stationed in Korea with her new husband, she found a baby Korean girl, later known as Wendy, left on their doorstep. They soon sought legal custody and eventually adopted her. Thus today Nam Mee is the mother of a nine-year-old Korean daughter. Nam Mee chose to have a hysterectomy because of her guilt in sending me away. Acceptance of Wendy as her own child has helped ease the pain and guilt she must have felt when she gave me up for adoption.

My interest in Nam Mee results not from a desire to return to her but from an interest in knowing many things about her—ranging from what is important to her to what her favorite color is. I am now able to reconcile having two sets of parents and two sources of important influence in my life and on my identity. By hearing Nam Mee talk of my childhood I can reclaim that part of my life, making me feel complete. Initially I was ambivalent about rekindling a relationship with my birth mother, but—had this opportunity not occurred—my mind would have continued wondering. I would have been filled with questions that would only have furthered self-doubt and confusion. By reconnecting with Nam Mee, I feel happier, more sure of myself, and ready to go on with my life.

And he wonderfully "went on with his life." Married to a lovely, re-sourceful woman, Mark and she are raising two dear daughters on the West Coast. Mark has a doctoral degree in clinical psychology and lives a fulsome life, reaching out to others. Nam Mee, currently living in Texas, has visited Mark's family and rejoices in her young grandchildren.

Acknowledgements

With special gratitude to those who read this manuscript in its evolving forms and made valuable suggestions.

www.ingramcontent.com/pod-product-compliance
Lightning Source LLC
Chambersburg PA
CBHW071636050426
42443CB00028B/3348